Ghosts in the Garden of England

by Alan Tigwell

Copyright, Alan Tigwell 2017

All rights reserved. No part of this book may be reproduced or used in any manner without the express written permission of the author.

Contents

Introduction 7
Penenden Heath, Maidstone 9
A21/ M25 18
Arlington, Ashford 20
Cobtree Manor Park, Aylesford 22
A20, Bearsted 24
North Street, Biddenden 26
Kits Coty House, Bluebell Hill 28
Weardale Manor, Toys Hill Road, Brasted Chart 31
Ordnance Street, Chatham 33
All Saints Hospital, Chatham 34
High Street, Cranbrook 36
Mill Street, East Malling 38
The Barrow House, Egerton 40
The Plough Inn, Eynsford, Dartford 42
South Road, Faversham 44
Shorncliffe Road, Folkestone 46
Ferndale Road, Gillingham 48
Lenham Road, Headcorn 51
Regent Way, Kings Hill 53
The Medway River, Larkfield 56
St Peter and St Paul's Church, Leybourne 58
St Mary's Church Ruins, Little Chart 61
Main Road, Longfield 65
Tonbridge Road, Maidstone 70
Tonbridge Road, Maidstone 72

Oakwood Hospital / Maidstone Hospital (Psychiatric Wing), Maidstone ..74

Victoria Road, Margate 76

Maidstone Road, Matfield 77

The Forgotten Gate, Park Road, Mereworth 80

Lossenham Lane, Newenden 82

Brookers Oast, The Hop Farm, Paddock Wood 85

Smarden Road, Pluckley 87

The Black Horse, Pluckley 89

Ransley Green, Ruckinge 91

Meadow Road, Rusthall 93

Springfield Road, Sittingbourne 95

High Street, Tenterden 97

College Avenue, Tonbridge 99

Goldsmid Road, Tonbridge 101

Greggs Wood Estate, Tunbridge Wells 105

Happy Valley, Tunbridge Wells 106

Silverdale Road, Tunbridge Wells 108

Monson Road, Tunbridge Wells 110

Grove Tunnel, Tunbridge Wells 112

Blackhurst Lane, Tunbridge Wells 115

The Bull Inn, West Malling 119

Lower Road, Woodchurch 122

Closing Thought 124

Introduction

Welcome to Ghosts in the Garden of England; a book of true ghost stories experienced by people in Kent. This county is commonly referred to as the garden of England due to the abundance of green spaces, hop gardens and fruit farms.

For those reading this from further afield, Kent is a county nestled in the South East of England, just South of London. The area is full of history and is home to Pluckley, a village listed in the Guinness Book of World Records as being the most haunted in England. I would personally dispute this; there are other villages in Kent which are far more haunted!

The stories in this book have never been previously published; you won't find them in other books or anywhere on the internet as they were all told directly to me by the people involved. There are also personal stories from me, which give details about some of the paranormal investigations I've been involved in over the last 20+ years. I have gone to great efforts to make sure the entirety of this book will be unique and new to you, rather than it being a retelling of well-known stories that have been around for many years.

In the pages of this book you will find some tales which are short and simple, and others which are more involved, such as the case I attended at Penenden Heath near Maidstone. The fact that these are the true-life stories of real people is what I believe makes them even more frightening and chilling.

As with anything written, slight editing has taken place to the stories, however I have ensured this was minimal to keep the experience true to life. All the stories are written the same way they were told to me. Where confidentiality has been requested, names have either been removed or replaced with another. However, the street and town of where the paranormal activity took place is the true location.

Now onto the stories; although they run in alphabetical order based on the town, to set the tone we'll start with my favourite story and the one that I was most involved in.

Best regards, Alan Tigwell

Penenden Heath, Maidstone
Sarah & Alan T

"One evening in January, I was watching a Disney movie with my husband and daughter in our bedroom when we heard someone knock at the door. I got up and went downstairs to answer the door but when I opened it, there was no-one there. I shrugged it off and came back upstairs, believing we may have heard someone knocking loudly at our neighbour's house. As soon as I sat down, we heard the knocking again. This time my husband went to see what was going on, but once again, when the door was opened, there was no-one there.

Convinced it was teenagers messing around, he closed the door but waited behind it, ready to swing it open when they came back. The door was made of solid wood, but as there was no window or spy hole to see who was outside, he pressed his ear up to the door and listened for someone walking across the gravel on our path which leads to the front door. The garden and road outside was silent and he couldn't hear anything. Just as he was about to give up and go back upstairs, there were three loud bangs against the door, making my husband literally jump out of his skin in fright. He hadn't heard anyone approaching the door which is why it frightened him so much.

He immediately swung the door open and stepped outside to confront the culprit, but there was no-one to be found. He couldn't understand what was going on, so he walked into the front garden to check behind some large bushes. He thought there could be a chance that was where the person was hiding, but still there was no one there. It was at that point the door behind him slammed, shutting him out of the house.

He ran to the door and started banging on it, shouting to us upstairs. My daughter and I could hear the commotion from our room, but were initially too frightened to come downstairs. When my husband stopped banging on the door, he then heard three slow, loud knocks coming from the inside, at which point he started screaming for us.

Hearing the terror in his voice, my daughter and I agreed we needed to get him back inside so we were all together. We came down the stairs, flung the door open and my husband, pale and obviously terrified, ran in and shut the door behind him. As he put the deadlock on the door, we saw there were long scratches on the inside panelling, deep into the wood. We huddled together, listening for movement in the house, but could only hear the movie which had been left on upstairs.

After a while, we searched the house for intruders but could find no-one. Thinking the police would consider us crazy, they were not called. Several days passed and things went back to normal. However, although we made light of the situation, there was a different feeling in the house, something which has always made me feel uncomfortable."

Update from Alan:

The above is a transcript of an answerphone message which was left for me. I contacted the caller and the following is what transpired.

My first visit to the property was to initially meet the parents and to get an understanding of the current situation. It would also give the opportunity for me to explain my approach to a situation of this nature and whether there was anything I could do to support the family. We all felt this course of action would be useful before I met the children.

They explained how they'd recently watched a TV drama series based on the case of the Enfield poltergeist, together with the supporting documentary where the investigator Maurice Grosse was interviewed. During the series, they had noticed some similarities between that case and the activity which was happening in their home. However, luckily they had not experienced a situation where any of their family had been possessed by a spirit.

After watching the programmes and researching online about the case in Enfield, their main concern of involving a paranormal investigator in their situation was one of anonymity. They had seen how the Enfield family was portrayed within the press and online and were obviously concerned about how publicity would affect their children. They made it clear they did not want to be in a situation where there was a potential for ridicule. I explained although I would be writing about some of the cases I had been involved in, their names and full address would never be revealed. I reassured them only the general location would be provided within the book or articles written. For the purposes of this book, I will refer to the parents as Sarah and Alex, and the children as Tom, aged 15 and Emma aged 12.

Reassured, Sarah and Alex went on to explain how the activity and events had begun and how it had escalated over the past few months, following a visit by a medium. This person was a friend of a friend and believed she was a psychic medium. During her visit, she had told the family there was an ancient angry spirit in the house and the only way to remove it would be to behave more aggressively than the spirit was.

Under the instruction of the medium, the family had started to leave camcorders running, took pictures around the house, shouted and ridiculed the spirit and even threw things at where they saw shadows moving in the house. Everything they did was based on being aggressive to the unseen visitor and the result was not a happy one.

Prior to the visit and instruction of the medium, the activity they had experienced only minor, things which made them look twice or be a little confused, such as shadows moving when there was no cause, lights blinking and unexplained noises such as scratching and knocking in the walls of the house. However, after the visit and change of approach towards it, Sarah and Alex explained rather than quiet the spirit into submission, they had actually angered it and increased the frequency and ferocity of the activity towards them and the children.

Both the children had told their parents independently about seeing a woman in their bedroom late at night. Although Emma had woken up and seen the figure on at least three occasions, it was Tom who had the marks to show. He had been woken up by his bed shaking and feeling a searing pain on his legs and arms. When he had run to his parents, they checked him over and found scratches all over his body. Tom also explained to his parents that when he woke up, there was a terrible smell, something like rotten eggs.

Sarah and Alex weren't immune to the spiritual attacks either. Alex explained how when he was having a shave one day, he had looked into the mirror to see the face of someone else looking back. It was his body, but his face had morphed into that of a hideous old woman with dark, leathery, wrinkled looking skin. A feeling of intense anger had suddenly overcome him, so he'd taken a step back, blinked and the face and negative feelings had gone; he was himself again.

Sarah recounted her story; she was in the kitchen cooking Sunday lunch when all of a sudden she'd received what appeared to be a punch in the stomach. She had doubled over and clutched where she'd been hit, only to feel a hard smack against her cheek, hard enough to knock her to the ground. When Alex came to see what the commotion was, he saw the red mark of a hand print on Sarah's cheek.

The spirit had definitely become physical with the whole family, parents and children alike. Everyone had experiences of being pushed around the house, including Emma who had been pushed down the stairs at one point. Luckily she had managed to grab hold of the bannister as she was falling, otherwise she could have received a serious injury.

Sarah also explained how she had been woken up one night and felt something breathe on her neck. Worried it was one of the children, she put the light on only to see the shape of an adult person standing behind the curtains. The curtains had then suddenly been pulled violently apart by an unknown force and nothing was there.

As Sarah, Alex and I were discussing their experiences, we heard a thud upstairs and all went to see what the cause was; we found a mug in the middle of one of the bedrooms. Sarah and Alex said it wasn't there earlier and they used the opportunity to show me round the upstairs of their home.

We were going back downstairs to continue our discussions, when we suddenly heard footsteps coming from the hall upstairs (the hall had stripped pine floorboards as did many of the rooms in the house). I went up on my own to look around, but no one could be found. I checked everywhere I could, even areas such as under beds and in the wardrobes.

When I asked Sarah and Alex about the history of the area, they told me they weren't aware of anything important. It was during this conversation that I suddenly felt someone slam their hands down on my shoulders. Sarah and Alex said they could see my shirt be depressed onto my shoulders and heard the slap of skin. Again, no-one was there, and no logical explanation was forthcoming. However, the atmosphere in the room felt oppressive and uncomfortable. Sarah and Alex explained this was the type of thing that happens to them regularly.

Soon we had drawn our conversation to a close and we all agreed I should meet the children together with the parents as a family for an introduction and then speak to them individually. We ended the meeting with me giving advice that as the suggested approach from the medium was clearly not working, any provocation of the entity should cease immediately, and no further interaction with the spirit should take place until we can work out what was going on.

We said our goodbyes at the door and Sarah and Alex went back into the house. As I was walking down the footpath, I looked back at the house and saw a figure in one of the upstairs bedrooms. As it was dark I couldn't make out specific features, but it definitely wasn't either of the occupants that I had just met. Almost straight after I had looked up, the figure moved back into the room, making the curtain fall back into place.

It wasn't until the second visit that the full story came out. This time I had returned to the house to interview the children. Emma who was 12, and Tom who was 15. As agreed with the parents in the earlier meeting, I saw them together as a family, then separately, but with their mother present in the room.

During the conversation with Tom, he was adamant he had no idea why the activity had started, but gave details of the activity he had witnessed which corresponded with the details I had already been given by his parents.

When talking to the daughter, Emma, she too initially denied any knowledge of the cause. We talked about a lot of general things; school, friends where she likes to play, but when Sarah mentioned that Emma used to like going to the play park on the Heath just down the road, she broke down in tears. It took some time for her mother to comfort her and convince her she wouldn't be in trouble if she told us the truth.

Emma went on to explain how she, her friend Becky, Tom and three of his friends had gone to the Heath one Sunday with one of Tom's friends father. While the boys were playing football on the field, Emma and Becky had spent time on the swings in the play park, chatting to each other.

After a while, Becky said she thought she'd seen Emma's mother over in the woods, watching them. Emma looked over but couldn't see anyone in that area. They continued their conversation for a while, but Becky was clearly unnerved. All of a sudden, Emma heard their names being called; she looked at Becky who had also stopped talking and was looking over into the woods again. When Emma followed her gaze, a woman stepped out from behind a tree over by the entrance to the woods. Although it was some distance away, they both recognised her as Emma's mother, Sarah, who was now waving to them and beckoning them over.

They left the enclosed play park and walked over to the woods where they'd seen the woman, who had now turned around and was walking into the woods. The girls hurried to catch up with her and ventured deeper into the trees. As they made ground on the woman, she turned to walk behind a tree, and disappeared from view.

Emma explained they felt drawn towards where they saw the woman disappear, and it was here they had stumbled across the burnt remnants of a fire. There was an unusual feeling around this area of the woods, which although wasn't very far from the play park, the sounds of playing children seemed muffled and difficult to hear. She said they had felt very isolated and alone.

In the charcoal remains of the fire, they found stones which appeared to have been placed in the fire when it had been alight. Emma picked up a stone and blew the white dust off; she could see the stone had unusual markings which looked as though it had been etched into the face and then the lines painted black. Becky also picked up a stone and did the same; the marking was almost identical.

Not wanting to be left alone in the woods, they put the stones in their pockets and looked around for Emma's mother. As no one could be seen, they returned to the play park thinking they would find her there. After waiting for a while, Tom came over to them and said they were all going home now, so they went with him, thinking Emma's mother had returned home. When Emma walked into the kitchen, she saw her mother washing dishes and asked why she hadn't waited for her; her mother had looked confused and said she had been at home all afternoon and that she hadn't been down to the park.

Sarah looked at me and confirmed she remembered the day and the strange question Emma had come home with. Sarah also realised that it was later that evening the first incident occurred in the house.

Emma said she still had the stone and went to her room to retrieve it from her jewellery box. Sarah asked me to take the stone away with me as she didn't want it in the house. Looking at the stone, it had an occult looking symbol etched into it. No trace of the fire was left on it.

Sarah, Alex and I met in the living room and the children went out to the back garden to play. They explained since their cessation of their aggressive stance, the entity had calmed and no further attacks on the family had taken place. Although there were still strange things happening in the house, they weren't hostile or frightening to the family. We agreed as things were calmer, we should follow up in a couple of weeks to make sure the removal of the stone wouldn't incite the spirit again.

I'm pleased to confirm the state of calm continued for the family and no further violent outbursts have taken place. As before, there is still paranormal activity in the house but the family is happy to live in peace with the entity. The entity does still appear to be upstairs in the home, as one day Alex was walking up the street behind one of his neighbours and saw them look up to the bedroom window, wave and walk on up the road. Alex looked up to the bedroom to see the curtains fall gently against the window, as if someone had just stepped backwards through them. As no-one was home, Alex asked the neighbour who he was waving at, and was told, "the old lady in the window who was waving at me".

It's worth noting a little about the history of Penenden Heath. Until the late 1800's, the area was mostly open heathland, extending to around 30 acres. It was used by the Saxons and Normans for public meetings, but more notoriously, the areas history goes hand in hand with death. This is because the heath was the site of public execution by hanging. In actual fact, there are two locations where gallows used to stand and what is now Heathfield Road, used to be called Hangman's Lane. Another macabre fact about the area is that when Maidstone Prison was being built, materials such as sand and earth were dug from the heath, close to the execution site, and transported into town. During this time, more than 300 skeletons were found, presumably the bodies of the executed.

Perhaps relevant to the case in hand, is that the Heath was also the execution site of six alleged witches in 1652. They were found guilty and sentenced to death. As was common at the time, two of the women pleaded that they were pregnant, but their reprieve came too late as they had already been hung at the Heath.

Penenden Heath has in the past been frequented by numerous paranormal investigation teams intent on communicating with the spirits of these witches or the other criminals who were executed on the heath. Looking at the investigation reports for many of them, it would appear they aren't aware of the true location of where the hangman's noose would have been as they spend their time on the playing field and woods behind. It is here that the stone was found by Emma.

A21/ M25
Alan T

Several years ago, I was part of an investigation into witchcraft and ritualistic practices taking place in Epping Forest in London.

On the way home at 3am, I was driving down the A21 towards Tunbridge Wells between the Bromley junction and the junction of the M25 when all of a sudden the headlights of a car appeared in my rear view mirror. Although this is not usually something that is out of the ordinary, I was a little surprised as the lights suddenly appeared as if just being switched on. Prior to this, I was also the only car on the road at such an early (or late!) time and the car appeared about 200 yards behind me. The road at this point is straight and we were already well past the junction; I certainly hadn't seen a car approaching me from the rear.

The car slowly came closer towards my car and sat literally on my bumper, a little too close for comfort. As I was about to put my foot down to pull away, the car pulled out into the middle lane to overtake.

I could see the car was white and appeared to be of an older style. I wasn't able to see the driver or any other occupants as the windows all appeared dark and there was no light coming from the inside. Today, you would assume the windows were tinted but for a car of this age, tinted windows were out of the ordinary.

The car started to overtake but slowed down just as it got to the blind spot of my mirrors. While I drove down the road, the car matched my speed. However, as we approached the M25 junction, I needed to move into the middle lane in order to continue down the A21. I slowed down to let the other car past, but again it matched my speed and slowed down as well, preventing me from changing lanes.

Eventually I had to put my foot down and pulled forward and away from the other car, enabling me to change lanes and continue on the correct road. The car remained behind me, at a more comfortable distance now, when all of a sudden, its headlights disappeared.

As I drove I watched in the rear-view mirror, waiting for the car to appear in the light of the street lamps behind me, but it never did. At that particular point of the road, there is nowhere for a car to pull in and at the speed we were both driving, it would have been impossible for the car to come to a halt before entering the light of the next street lamp. The car never appeared to me again on the journey home.

Since then, I've heard of other drivers having a similar experience on this stretch of road and every time the car disappears at the same place.

Arlington, Ashford
Thomas S

Several years ago when I was 14, I was staying at the home of my friend, Stephen. It was a Saturday night and we were watching TV till quite late. It was nothing out of the ordinary and certainly nothing scary as my friends mum wouldn't let us watch that type of thing, no matter how many times he asked her.

Once the film had ended we headed upstairs to his room and got into our beds. He had a bunk bed and as the guest, I got the top bunk. We were both playing our hand-held consoles, Gameboys, for a while. When it got to about midnight, his mum came into the room and told us it was time to go to sleep.

His mum switched the light off and the only illumination was from the street lights outside, casting a dim orange glow into the room. Although the curtains were closed, the light shone through the thin material. It was very dim and only just illuminated parts of the room. It wasn't often I was allowed to stay up this late so I felt exhausted and it wasn't long before I was dropping off to sleep.

I could hear Stephen in the bunk underneath breathing and slightly snoring; it was clear he was already asleep and the room was otherwise silent. I could hear the TV in the living room downstairs, his parents still up and awake, but they had turned the volume down so not to keep us awake.

In the state between being awake and asleep, I suddenly became very aware of something I can only describe as being 'off' in the room. It was August and the temperature in the day was uncomfortably hot. The nights were also warm but not uncomfortably so. However, as I lay there, the temperature of the previously warm room dropped. It had dropped drastically to the point where I now snapped out of the almost asleep state as I now started to shiver with the cold. I pulled the duvet up around me to try to warm myself up.

As I tried to fall back asleep, I heard a very feint noise. At first I thought it was coming from the TV in the living room downstairs, but then I realised what the noise was. It wasn't the sound of talking from a TV show, it was the sound of crying. I also realised it wasn't coming from downstairs, it was actually in the room.

The cry was very soft, as if someone was trying not to be heard. Thinking it was Stephen, I looked over from my top bunk down to the bunk below. I could just see Stephen in the light from outside, and he was clearly asleep and definitely not crying.

I laid back on my bed, wondering what was going on. The crying continued and I realised where it was coming from. It was emanating from the corner of the room, next to Stephens bookshelf. The large stack of shelves didn't quite fit into the corner of the room and it left a small gap between itself and the wall. It was here that the sounds were coming from.

Some people may say that it may have been my sudden fear, that I was tired or that there wasn't much light in the room, but I swear I saw a shape in the corner of the room, in the space. It was like a dark hunched figure.

As the room got colder, I felt my duvet start to slowly be pulled off the bunk. I grabbed hold of it and held it tightly, terrified at what was happening. I could feel something pulling at it.

At this point, a smell came over me, it was a terrible rancid smell and reminded me of when we found a dead fox in the woods the summer before. It made me want to gag and hold my nose, but I didn't as that would mean me losing my grip on the duvet.

As my terror and fear grew, I swear I saw movement from the corner of the room. All of a sudden, the pulling of the duvet stopped, the smell was gone and the shape from the corner of the room dissipated. The temperature also went back to normal within a matter of seconds. All that remained was my fear and a cold sweat on my forehead. That was the last time I ever stayed at my friend's house.

Cobtree Manor Park, Aylesford
Sophie R

When I was younger, probably about eight or nine, my mum used to take me to the local park in Aylesford during the day, and my dad would meet us while he was on his lunch break. On one of these days, my sister and I went there and were playing in one of the open areas and decided it would be a good idea to play hide and seek. My sister was the hider and I was the seeker.

Once I finished counting down, I started to look for her in the area we were playing. Unable to find her, I decided she was most probably in the woods which form a large part of the park and was next to where we had been playing. My mum was sat on the picnic blanket reading a book, so being the bundle of energy I was at that age, I ran in thinking I would quickly find her hiding behind one of the large trees.

I looked and looked for some time but still couldn't find any trace of her. It was at that point that I realised I'd wandered further into the woods than I'd intended and had gotten lost. Being only eight years old, I was terrified and began to cry. I felt somebody come over and I looked up to see an old lady standing in front of me. Seeing her kind, smiling face, I immediately felt a sense of calm and believed everything would be alright. She asked why I was crying, so I explained that I was lost, and I didn't know where my mum was.

She reassured me that everything was going to be OK and held my hand. I remember thinking at the time how cold her hand felt in mine, even though it was a warm day in the summer. She asked me what my mother looked like, if I could remember which direction I came into the woods from and other questions of that nature. She then asked me if I had seen any of the animals yet. I had no idea what she was talking about, so I asked, "which animals?" She then pointed and said, "is that your mother?" I looked and saw my mum and sister running towards me, with worried looks on their faces.

I let go of the old lady's hand and hugged my mum, who began to tell me off for coming into the woods on my own. I said to her that it was OK because the old lady had looked after me, and that I needed to thank her. I looked behind me, but the lady had gone. My mum looked puzzled and said, "what old lady?" I explained about the lady who had come to my aid and held my hand until she found me. My mum said that when she had seen me and ran to me, I had been standing there on my own; there had been no-one else around.

It's something I've always remembered and looking back in hindsight, I now know that the clothes she was wearing were very old fashioned and out of context for the time. I've investigated the history of the park and seen old pictures of when this park was Maidstone Zoo. It was closed in the 1950's and had many animals such as elephants, chimpanzees, emus, a lion and exotic birds. It was even bombed during the war but I'm not sure if anyone died when this happened. There was no way the old lady could have walked away without being seen, and the clothes in the pictures I saw were very similar to what the lady wore. I'm convinced she was a spirit of a time when the park was originally the zoo.

The only building still left from when the zoo existed is the Elephant House which is now in a rather dilapidated state but once housed two elephants called Gert and Daisy. There is also a secret hidden location in the park where the graves of some of the animals can be found.

A20, Bearsted
David F

One evening my girlfriend went to a party at one of her friends' houses. I was due to pick her up once it had finished, but as I'd never met the friend or knew where she lived (although I knew which village) I was going to rely on inputting her postcode into my satnav.

When it came time to collect her, she sent me a text with the postcode, so I set off on my way, which took me down the M20 towards a village called Leeds. This village is where Leeds Castle is located; I had been there before, so I knew which junction I would have to leave the motorway on.

As I was passing the Maidstone junction, I noticed the satnav was going to take me off the M20 early and connect me to the A20 which goes through Bearsted; this road runs parallel to the motorway. I knew this was a junction too early, so I was going to carry on and let the satnav automatically re-adjust the route on the way. However, as I neared the junction I started to feel a surge of anxiety; it's as if something was telling me to get off the motorway. I don't usually have feelings like this, so I decided to trust the satnav and followed the route it was telling me, even though I knew it would take longer.

About 5 minutes later, I was driving along the A20 and I saw a man in the distance standing on a corner. As I drove closer, I saw he was one of my friends, Alex. At the time, I thought it was strange as he was dressed completely out of character for him. He was wearing smart back trousers, a black shirt and a red tie. Normally he would be dressed in jeans and a t shirt.

As I drove past, I opened my window and waved and shouted at him, but he just started at me. His eyes were strange, vacant and emotionless but they followed me as I went past. I went on my way, feeling a little uncomfortable at the encounter and the way he had looked at me as I went past. I soon found the house where the party had been and collected my girlfriend.

As we were driving back and about to join the motorway, there was a lot of police activity and we were told the motorway was closed. We had to come back on the same road I had driven earlier, and I was a little anxious as to whether I would see Alex again. As we drove past the corner where I'd previously seen him, there was no-one there.

We put the radio on to see if there was any news on why the motorway was closed and we learnt there had been a terrible fatal accident at the same time I would have been driving along it earlier that evening. The traffic report told us a car had been travelling on the northbound carriageway but had lost control and had somehow flipped over the central reservation into oncoming traffic. I had never been so grateful that my satnav had sent me on a different route! Had I not left the motorway when I had, I would have been involved in the accident.

When my girlfriend heard this, I was shocked to hear her say she hoped Alex wasn't caught up in the accident as he had been at the party with his new girlfriend but had left before I arrived. She described him as wearing the same smart clothes I saw him in earlier; he had made an extra special effort as he was trying to impress his new girlfriend.

The next day we received some terrible news; it was Alex's car that had lost control and caused the accident and he had been declared dead at the scene. There was no logical reason for me to have seen him standing on the corner of the road I was driving on, or why my satnav took me off the motorway when it did. I still can't explain it to this day.

North Street, Biddenden
Stuart E

I'd been doing some house sitting for some friends while they were on holiday, to prevent their dog, Petra, from being put into a kennel for several weeks. During most visits, I'd felt uncomfortable in the property, as if there was a heaviness in the air and I'd even heard noises of movement upstairs a few times. The uneasiness I felt wasn't a new experience, I'd felt it before while in the house; even when my friends were here.

Initially I believed Petra was wandering the rooms and causing the noises, but upon inspection, she was found to be asleep in her basket. Each time I checked, the cause of the noises could not be identified as there was no-one else in the property.

On one occasion in particular, I had arrived at the house at dusk. Petra appeared distressed and would not walk past the stairway. She kept looking up to the landing on the second floor.
Concerned, I asked Petra what was up and started to show her attention. At that point I heard a noise coming from the top of the stairs. Startled, I looked up the stairs to see a tennis ball come bouncing down them.

It rolled behind the open front door and Petra, who would normally never let a tennis ball get the better of her, watched it roll past. She then looked back up the stairs and stepped aside as if avoiding someone.

Believing there was an intruder in the property, I had taken out my camera phone and had begun taking pictures, even though nothing could be seen on the stairs now the ball had rolled past. To my amazement, the front door swung shut on its own behind me. Petra the dog moved back and seemed to be watching someone go back upstairs.

I followed the dog's gaze and saw a flash of the upper body of a woman on the landing looking right at me; she had dark hair and a pulled up, white high collar ruffled blouse. I only saw her for a moment as she was gone as quickly as she had appeared, but she seemed to have a kind face and I didn't think there was any malicious intent.

In an effort to communicate, I spoke out "Hello, I saw you and what you did. Thank you for that. I'm Stuart and this is Petra." As I did so, the top of the staircase developed a white haze that boiled mid-air for a moment then vanished.

I continued, "I feel like this was your home some time ago. Petra and her family live here now, and dearly love this home as you do."

Unfortunately, I didn't observe anything else while I stayed at the house, but the atmosphere seemed to change and the oppressiveness dissipated. For some reason, all the pictures on my camera phone were corrupted.

When my friends returned from their holiday, we discussed what had happened. The owner reassured me that the ghost frequently made an appearance, usually around Petra.

My friend admitted he had also tried to communicate using a wide range of methods, such as lighting candles and asking for the flames to be blown out and also eliciting wraps and knocks from around the house. He was successful in several of these sessions, but unfortunately nothing was ever recorded.

Kits Coty House, Bluebell Hill
Andy W

A bit of a strange name, but Kits Coty House is a Neolithic monument and a chambered long barrow on bluebell hill. A long barrow is basically a burial mound with a chamber inside made of wood or stone. There are several of these long barrows in the area and are commonly referred to as the Medway Megaliths. This monument has three large stones standing upright with another large circular stone sitting on top. It is all fenced off and is an English Heritage site.

In terms of who is actually buried here, no one knows. The general consensus is that 'Kit' refers to someone called Catigern who was in a battle against the Saxons in 455.

Onto my story. My two brothers and I love to learn about historical places, particularly if they are meant to be haunted. Kits Coty has quite the reputation for paranormal events such as the re-enactment of battles, ghosts of Roman soldiers and other folklore. We had talked about coming here for some time but had never gotten round to it. My brother was due to leave for university at the end of August, so we decided it was now or never, so we planned our trip and all bundled into my older brothers car.

Parking at Bluebell Hill was a nightmare, we had the choice of leaving the car up in a parking area, but then had to walk down the edge of a very busy and fast flowing road or squeeze the car in against the side of the lane at the bottom of the hill. We opted for the safer parking area, safer for us, but not necessarily for the car! We crossed the road and found the entrance to the footpath up to Kits Coty.

The footpath up to the burial place was steep. None of us are particularly athletic; I hate to say it, but we struggled and were all out of breath quite quickly.

We had looked at the site on Google maps so knew where we were going, about a quarter of a mile up the hill to where the stones were situated. It was along this footpath that our experience of something paranormal started. Being the ever-intrepid ghost hunters, we had our audio recorders and video cameras recording our expedition up the hill, just in case we caught anything. I'm glad we did.

As we were nearing the gap in the hedge where we could walk through to the stones, something unexplained happened. I suffer from tinnitus, a medical condition which causes a high-pitched ringing to heard in my ears, something similar to when a tuning fork is rung. Bizarrely for me, mine comes on or gets worse when there is an electrical field nearby, such as when a TV is on standby mode.

As we were getting to the point of the hill where we would veer off the path, my tinnitus started and I had an incredibly high pitch noise start ring in my ears. The next thing I knew was waking up after being flat on the floor, next to my brothers who were also apparently waking up at the same time.

To start with, we were all in a state of confusion and we just stared at each other not knowing what had just happened. I saw the camcorders on the ground, still recording us as we gathered our thoughts, stood up and brushed the dirt and dust from our clothes.

We grabbed the camcorders and rewound the recording to see what happened. It turned out we had been unconscious for about fifteen minutes. The recording showed us walking up the hill, huffing and puffing with the exertion, and then the video briefly went fuzzy with static, something you don't normally see on modern day digital recordings. It's at this point we all fall down, all at the same time and the camcorder hits the ground and falls onto its side. It still had a good view of us, lying there unconscious. It's a weird feeling to see yourself doing something you have no recollection of!

About five minutes later, some sort of mist flows across the path, over our bodies and seems to head toward the stones and the field beyond the left side of the path. The strange thing about this mist is that there seems to be differing variations of density, as if some of it were partially solid. It's not something I can explain and it's difficult to see on the video, but at one point it looks as though something knocks into one of my brothers and makes his body shift. When we saw this, we looked at him and realised he was holding his shoulder; he pulled his t-shirt to one side and we all saw a red mark and a graze which he swears wasn't there before, and wasn't the side of his body which hit the ground when he fell.

We also rewound the audio recorder to the point where we fell down; we can clearly hear the noises of us falling and the recorder hitting the ground, but nothing else out of the ordinary is on the recording.

When we had collected our thoughts and as we were practically there already, we decided to continue our journey to the stones. We took a good look around, but there was no mist in the field or around the stones and couldn't see anything that would have accounted for our experience. I know people will say we passed out because we were out of breath, but all of us at the exact same time? I don't think so! It also doesn't explain about the mist and whatever knocked into my brother.

Weardale Manor, Toys Hill Road, Brasted Chart
Jean S

My story is of an experience I had while on a ghost hunt at Weardale Manor. The manor is now a ruin and you can only see the foundations of what was once the house. Close to this, there is a large memorial stone. The land where it is located is on Toys Hill which is mostly woodland and is managed by the National Trust. The area is recommended as a circular walk which links two other National Trust properties in the area; Emmetts Garden and Chartwell.

The previous day I had visited the area, just so I would be prepared and could get my bearings on the night time ghost hunt. The only thing out of the ordinary that I'd experienced during the day was in the corner of the ruin. Someone had put a dream catcher in one of the old trees. I'd tried to take a picture of it using my smartphone, but every picture I took came out with a weird glitch; such as a rainbow effect, digital errors or the picture itself stretched so much that it was unrecognisable. It was the only time the camera in the phone had ever taken pictures like this!

When I returned the following day for the ghost hunt, I was met by around ten people and we were led in the darkness to the same spot I had found the day before. We were given some equipment and after a short explanation, we were told to wander the grounds of the ruin and see if we could communicate with the spirits. Most people had come as a couple and they went off in different directions; as I came on my own, I was left to wander alone. There are no lights in the ruin or the woods, and we were out in the country so to say it was dark, really doesn't do it justice! We each had a torch with us so we were reliant on the light they gave.

After a while, something caught the corner of my eye in the lower section of the ruin. I walked down the steps and over to the right-hand corner of would have previously been a room. There was a footpath that led into the woods and weeds, nettles and brambles had made it look like a circular hole into the darkness. I saw movement again and spotted a rabbit running away and into the woods. From behind me, I distinctly felt someone as if someone had put their hand onto my left shoulder. Not expecting someone to do that, I was startled for a moment. I turned around to see what the person wanted, but there wasn't anyone there. All the rest of the group were in the upper section of the ruin, away from where I was standing.

Shocked, it took a moment to collect my thoughts and stop myself from shaking; I went up to the team leader and explained what had happened. He called the group over and recounted a story of his own which was almost identical. It turns out, in the same spot he also had someone touch his shoulder, but like my experience, when he turned around, there was no one there.

The conversation continued until someone else in the group raised their torch and illuminated the large memorial stone. Both that person and their partner whispered "look" and pointed over in the direction of their torch beam. We all looked around and although there was movement in the trees, could see nothing. The couple explained they had seen something move on the stone and when they shone their torch onto it, saw a dark shadowy person clinging to the top of the stone, who disappeared shortly after being illuminated by the beam of light. We all rushed over to the area and shone our torches into the woods, but could see nothing.

Ordnance Street, Chatham

Claire D

One night I had a tough time sleeping in my bedroom due to my husbands snoring, so I went into the living room to sleep on the sofa. I awoke at around 2am to see a woman standing over me with a blue aura surrounding her. She seemed to have a sad expression on her face and looked as though she had been crying.

She extended her hand towards my face, at which point I recoiled; I tried to grab her arm or wrist to stop her from touching me, but was unable to. I remember trying three times but couldn't feel a thing, at which point I yelled out for my husband, who was still sleeping upstairs. The woman started to move away from me and left the room into the hallway towards the stairs.

My husband must have heard me as he switched the upstairs light on, and I heard him start to come down the staircase; he then cried out and I heard him tumble down some of the stairs. I immediately got up and went to his aid.

I found him at the bottom of the stairs and although he had not injured himself, he was clearly shaken and pale. He explained he must have tripped in his rush to get to me after I had called for him. I asked if he had seen the woman, but he advised he had not.

To help calm me down, we both checked the house, looking in each room, but nothing out of the ordinary could be seen. All doors and windows were locked from the inside so my husband felt as though it may have been my mind playing tricks on me, having just woken up. We went to bed, but I was unable to sleep.

Ever since that night while being in the living room late at night, I always get the feeling something or someone is watching me.

All Saints Hospital, Chatham
Tim V

My mum had an experience when she wasn't very well and needed to have a number of small operations in hospital. She was in one of the wards getting over the procedure and although not in pain, was having difficulty getting to sleep. There were a few other patients having trouble sleeping too.

A nurse came over and asked if she was OK and offered to make her a cup of tea, to which my mum accepted. My mum explained there was something about the nurse that wasn't quite right but couldn't work out what it was, so she thought no more of it. The nurse left, and my mum waited.

It was quite some time before the nurse came back, probably in the region of an hour. Still having trouble getting to sleep, my mum gladly accepted the tea from the nurse. It was at this point my mum realised the nurse was wearing a different design of uniform to the rest of the staff she had seen during the day; it was the type she saw on nurses when she was a little girl. Perplexed, she asked the nurse about the uniform but never received a response, as the nurse carried on with her duties seeing to the other patients. Comforting those who were in pain or bringing tea to those unable to sleep. After drinking her tea, which tasted delicious, she fell asleep.

The next morning, when the nurse on duty came over to see how she was, my mum asked who the kind lady was on duty the previous night. She described the woman and her uniform, but the nurse said there was no-one who matched that description who worked in this ward, let alone who was on duty during the night. The nurse was a little blunt with my mum (the complete opposite of the treatment she had received during the night!) and just said how the painkillers must have made her see things. The tea cup was still on the stand next to my mums bed, so she knew that wasn't the case.

My mum is never one to let things go, so she went and spoke to some of the other patients who had been comforted by the unknown nurse during the night. Bizarrely, each one of them described the lady completely differently, including the colour of her skin and hair! The only thing that remained consistent were the descriptions of the uniform she was wearing.

She never did get to the bottom of who she was, or why everyone had a different account of what she looked like. However, more than one of the patients were convinced a kind spirit had visited them in their hour of need.

The hospital has quite a history. It was previously the Medway Union Workhouse and was built in 1849. This workhouse is commonly believed to be the one mentioned in the Charles Dickens' novel, Oliver Twist. The hospital itself has now been redeveloped although apparently some of the buildings were left intact rather than knocking the whole site down. I wonder if any of the residents have seen the ghost?

High Street, Cranbrook
Kelly P

I lived in a property in the High Street of Cranbrook for many years while I was growing up and my parents still live there now. I would sometimes feel there was a negative presence in my bedroom at night. I didn't get the sense that it was evil, but it was clearly unfriendly towards me. I didn't know whether the presence was male or female, but I had the distinct impression that it was looking at me during the night from one of the corners of the room.

I also discovered as a little girl that I would lose things which had great sentimental meaning. On my 13th birthday, my parents gave me a ring which belonged to my grandmother, to whom I was very close. One time I had a friend in my room and made the mistake of mentioning that my ring was my prized possession. As soon as I said it, I realised that I shouldn't have vocalised my feelings about the ring.

That night when I went to sleep, I clutched the right tightly in my hand. When I woke up the next day, my hand was still clenched in the same position but the ring was gone. My parents and I searched the room, but the ring was never found. I was devastated. Throughout my childhood, things like this happened all the time.

When I turned 18, I moved out of the house as I just couldn't bear the feelings and negative atmosphere each and every night in my room. However, about three years ago I had to come back to the house to stay due to a water leak in my own home. That night I ended up having to stay in my old bedroom for the first time in 11 years, and even after all that time, the bad feelings were still there. I was convinced I still felt a presence in the room over towards the door.

Having remembered the missing items from my youth, I realised I had all my personal items such as my mobile phone, my purse and jewellery in my handbag just left on the chair in the corner of the room. Although concerned, I realised I was worrying for no reason and that I should leave the items where they were. Shortly after, I fell asleep. When I awoke in the morning, I was glad to find all my belongings still in my bag where I had left them the night before.

About a week later, I was showing my friend some pictures of my new puppy on my mobile phone when I discovered six new pictures. Six pictures which terrified me. The pictures were of me, sleeping in the bed in my old bedroom taken from the angle of where I always perceived the presence was in the room.

Mill Street, East Malling
Mark B

My house has been in my family for many years and dates back a few hundred years. It was left to me by my parents when they passed away and it's the place I call home, having been raised as a child in its walls. We live in a lovely section of East Malling, quite close to the church. The activity we experienced has been going on for as long as I can remember but seemed to intensify when my girlfriend moved in. We are now married so at least the activity didn't scare her away!

One example of the type of experiences I have of living in a haunted house was one night my girlfriend and I were upstairs in my bedroom. The activity started off in a relatively quiet way; down in the kitchen we have quarry tiles and I could hear footsteps coming and going. I asked my girlfriend if she had heard that, to which she initially said she couldn't, but after a while, she said she could also hear the footsteps.

We could also hear clinking down there too, it was like someone was either putting the china away into the cupboard, or clinking two cups together. The noises got louder and louder and it started to sound as though it was approaching my bedroom upstairs. I know people usually say they feel the temperature drop when ghosts or spirits are around, but for me, the room gets quite hot! Having had this type of experience before, I reassured my girlfriend and opened the door. As I expected, the hall was empty and the noises immediately stopped.

Sometimes the ghost is mischievous and hides important documents or things like keys, only to have them reappear in the most obvious place after we've turned the house upside down. It's frustrating but something I've learned to live with.

We also hear tapping going on within the walls. It doesn't always happen at night, it can take place during the day as well. I've had the pest control people out to make sure its not mice, insects or rodents in the wall cavities, but they've reassured me they couldn't find anything. Sometimes the sound of tapping comes into the room itself and I occasionally play a game with the spirit by mimicking the number of taps it makes or asking questions and getting taps as a response. I've tried to get the ghost to give us the lottery numbers but I've not been that lucky yet!

The Barrow House, Egerton
Ryan M

About a five-minute walk away from where my friends and I live we have a local pub. Although it has changed hands several times, we have always made good friends with the staff there. It's existed for hundreds of years and there is a lot of history to it. When you first walk in you don't feel a strange atmosphere, but you do notice the age of the pub and the staff try to keep things as original as possible.

A few years ago, we were talking to the staff and we got onto the topic of the paranormal. They explained that when the pub is closed and the customers go home it usually takes them an hour to tidy up, collect the glasses and make the pub neat again (the pub has a cleaner who comes each morning to fully clean the place).

Sometimes they stop for a drink before going home. When they do this, they occasionally hear what sounds like glasses being collected. At the time they are the only people in the building. The amount of glasses being collected makes it sound like someone is walking around collecting them off the tables behind them. When they turn around to see where the noises are coming from, there is never anyone there, nor are there ever any glasses on the tables in the first place as they had already been collected. They believe it's the work of a previous landlord who may have died there some time ago.

This isn't the only thing that happens at the pub though; above the bar are a number of lights which flicker at strange intervals. No matter how many times they have changed the bulbs the problem still continues. They have gone to great lengths to try to identify what the cause could be and have called numerous electricians, but all have confirmed there is no issue with the wiring or electric circuits and there is no cause for alarm or concern.

They explained to me that at one point in the past, a psychic fair was hosted at the pub. One of the people who had a stall there attempted to communicate with a spirit via the flickering lights. They had quite a conversation with the spirit, but over time the content of the conversation has been forgotten.

My girlfriend also experienced something strange here as well. After having a few drinks, she needed to use the toilet. She told me there was no-one else in there; all the toilet stalls were empty and their doors were open. She chose the cubicle at the end of the line and when she was finishing up, but hadn't opened the cubicle door, she felt a hard tap on shoulder which was followed with a short cough, which sounded as though it came from a man. She screamed, threw the door open and leapt out of the cubicle. She spun around to see who it could have been, but there was no-one there; she was alone in the room.

I remember the look on her face when she came back to our table; she was white and trembling. She never came back to the pub again!

The Plough Inn, Eynsford, Dartford
Alan T

The village of Eynsford is very old, dating back prior to 864 when it was first mentioned in writing. The Plough Inn is one of the older buildings remaining in the village and dates to the 16th century. It was here that I was participating in an investigation as part of a team, as there had been several reports of activity and the landlord was interested in finding out more.

He explained how there were tales of a ghostly woman who allegedly haunts the outside of the pub and has been seen tapping the window with a coin. Regulars have joked about hearing the tapping when its time for another round! The landlord also told us he believes there is a poltergeist present in the pub, as items are regularly moved when no-one is around, or they disappear altogether.

While we were filming in the restaurant upstairs, the camcorder was focussed on the lead investigator. A well-known psychic, he was calling out to see if any spirits would make contact. The camcorder I was using was fitted to a tripod and was filming in night shot mode with an additional infrared illuminator to make the picture clearer in the dark room.

In the viewfinder I witnessed a dark shape cross the room towards the other investigators. We stopped and viewed the video to try to find out what it was. In the video we could clearly see the shape of a person crossing the room, but at the time, no-one was moving and all the investigators were accounted for.

We all discussed the potential causes and agreed the most probable answer was one of the investigators had crossed in front of the infrared illuminator during the recording. This could have cast the shadow into the room which would have then been caught on video. The only problem with this explanation was that everyone said they hadn't been moving at the time. We continued the investigation with no further paranormal events, but by the end of the night the whole team was questioning whether what we caught on camera earlier in the night had a natural explanation.

However, when I returned to the Plough Inn several months later for a meal, I discussed the previous event with our waitress who had been absent on the night of the investigation. When I told her about the shadow being recorded, she smiled and explained that she was well aware of the upstairs restaurant being haunted by the figure of a man who crosses the restaurant and descends the stairs. She said that she had witnessed the figure in the room when she was clearing up one night.

I realised the lead investigator was standing at the top of the stairs when we had made the recording. Is it possible that we had in fact recorded the ghost rather than the shadow of an investigator?

South Road, Faversham
Ann B

A resident in this street believes she has witnessed and experienced several unexplained phenomena over the years while living here. She told me about one experience which was shared with her mother, who had a background as a scientist and did not believe in the paranormal. During this particular occurrence they were both frightened to the point where they had to call the police.

She explained, "About three years ago, we bought a new house. At the time, my parents thought they had a fantastic deal, as even though the house was for sale for much less that it was worth, the owners accepted an offer which was even lower.

The night we moved into the house, my dad had been called inti work to resolve an issue, so we decided to celebrate by having a meal out at a restaurant in a nearby village. My mother was getting ready in the bathroom, I was in my bedroom and I could also hear my little sister in her room watching the television.

At this point, we heard our dog start barking and whining in the kitchen, to which my mum asked me to go and check the kitchen door had not been shut accidentally. As I came out of my room, I saw our dog stand up from a lying position in the hall and scurry into my parents' bedroom. I proceeded to tell my mum that the dog had already come upstairs by herself, at which point I again heard the sound of a dog crying downstairs. I ran into the bathroom with my mum and asked whether she had also heard that, but as I did we both heard a man's whistling coming from downstairs.

We pulled each other close and my mum whispered to me, pointing towards the staircase, "do you hear that too?" We both ran to my sisters room who was still watching TV and was oblivious to what was happening, my dog soon followed.

My mum tried to calm the situation by telling us it was probably my dad getting home from work early. We decided to call his mobile phone just to be safe, but when we spoke to him, he told us he was still at the office. At that point we heard more noises from downstairs which sounded like someone running between the rooms. We told my dad what was happening; he said to hang up and call the police and he would come home straight away.

My dad got home just as the police arrived but by that point the noises had stopped. They checked all over the house, making sure the doors and windows were secure but as there was no evidence of a break-in, there wasn't anything they could do. However, one of the officers mentioned they had been called to the house several times in the past by the previous owner, under very similar circumstances.

Shorncliffe Road, Folkestone

Karen G

The house I spent my mid teenage years in was a relatively new house, so I never expected to have any sort of paranormal activity to take place. I always assumed that sort of thing happened in houses which were a couple of hundred years old. I was definitely wrong! Shortly after moving in, my experiences started and they happened to me all the time. As you can imagine, anything paranormal or ghostly happening to a 13-year-old child was absolutely terrifying.

Some of the experiences I had were your general run of the mill type of experience, the type of stuff you hear about all the time. Things like hearing footsteps walking around an upstairs room when I was alone; I'd call out for my mum or dad thinking they'd come home without me realising and there would be no answer. I would run up the stairs and as expected, nothing or nobody would be there. There would also be doors slamming behind me; I'm not talking about just gently closing, I'm talking about absolutely slamming! I may have been young, but I knew enough about life to at least consider the effects of the pipes, wind or gravity. Even so, there was never a logical explanation.

One night I was lying on my bed; it was a solid pine bed which had a headboard and a board at the end of the bed too. All of a sudden the entire bed shifted with a loud bang, as if someone had run against the footboard with all of their might. It was hit with enough force to nearly throw me off the bed! I jumped off and looked around the room and under the bed, even though my heart was pounding and I was terrified. I have no idea where I mustered the courage to do that! I knew I hadn't dreamt or imagined it, the bed had definitely moved as I could see the marks in the carpet where the legs of the bed had originally been; they were about two inches away from where the bed was now situated. I tried to re-enact what had happened and the only way I could get the same noise and make the bed move like it did, was to hit the footboard with all my strength.

When I lived there, I always got a feeling that I wasn't wanted, I seemed to be the focus of attention of whatever spirit lived in the house. Although this attention did seem to be hostile towards me, I was never hurt or physically injured. Even so, I was glad when we moved due to my mum getting a new job further away. It was actually my older cousin that bought the house from us.

When we visited, I would ask her whether anything had happened; I'd previously been honest with her about my experiences, as I didn't want a family member to buy the house without knowing about the ghost (my parents weren't happy when they found out what I had said!) but she also had strange things happen and would tell me the stories; one of which I witnessed while visiting her on my own one day.

She is a great cat lover and has a number of them, four, in fact. We were sat in the living room one day and all four of the cats were in their favourite spots dotted around the room. The one in the corner of the room suddenly bolted out the room and into the kitchen which made the rest of them jump. The remaining three all stared up to the closed living room door (there were two exits, one to the kitchen where the first cat had darted and the other out into the hall but this door was closed). They stared at the closed door; as another cat made a swift exit into the kitchen, the other two arched their backs, hissing at the door. They too made a run for the kitchen when the door handle started to jiggle and turn.

My cousin casually got up, opened the door and sat back down with a smile. She looked at me and very calmly just said that the ghost didn't like having this door closed and that although she had come to terms with living in a haunted house, her cats hadn't yet!

Ferndale Road, Gillingham
Brian N

I recently saw an article on black eyed children; they seem to be a popular thing in the world of the paranormal at the moment. The stories reminded me of some strange encounters I had outside a place my wife and I used to rent in Ferndale Road.

There was nothing extraordinary about the road or place we were renting, just your average road with houses on one side and an enclosed area opposite, I suppose you'd call them gardens; it wasn't a park or anything like that, but it was a public place and they were opposite our home so we were glad we could look out of the window at them. We were also very close to the railway line so it was good to have some greenery to muffle the noise of the trains.

One evening, I was returning home from work and as I was walking up the street, in the distance I saw a girl dressed in a black dress go into the gardens. It was dark and quite late in the evening, so it was a little out of the ordinary to see a girl of what I guessed to be 8 or 9 walking around the streets on her own. I was some distance off, so by the time I got to where the entrance to the gardens are, she was gone and I couldn't see anyone. I assumed a parent or someone was already in the garden when I spotted the girl and they had gone on their way.

Bizarrely, I felt a little bit unsettled as I continued to walk past the gardens; I felt goosebumps on my arms and the air had a chill to it which I hadn't felt before. I couldn't explain why I felt like that, it was as if a certain degree of fear had been conjured inside me. I hurried across the road and into my home.

A little while later, my wife got home from her job. Once she had come into the house and took her coat off, she asked me whether I'd seen the strange girl in the gardens over the road. Since coming into the house, I'd closed the curtains and hadn't looked out, so I went into our living room and took a look out of the window. Sure enough, there was a girl standing in the gardens opposite. It was dark so the only light was from the street lights, but they illuminated the gardens quite well and I could tell it seemed to be the same girl in the black dress that I'd seen earlier. She was just standing there, facing our house. Again, my goosebumps came back and I quickly closed the curtains.

I explained I'd seen her earlier going into the gardens but wasn't there when I walked past. My wife told me that when she was parking the car, she'd seen the girl just standing in the gardens, apparently on her own. My wife is a very caring and loving person, who would do anything for anyone, so she was obviously concerned the girl was alone in the dark and could be lost, so she got out of the car and walked over to her. Standing in front of the girl, my wife had asked if she was alright and whether she needed assistance. My wife explained to me how the girl had just stared at her with huge dark eyes and didn't answer. My wife had asked a couple of other times before becoming a little scared at how the girl was looking at her, so she had come into the house.

We looked out of the window again and the girl was still there, staring back at us. I said to my wife that we couldn't just leave here there on her own, so we both agreed to go out and see if she would talk to us this time. We left the house together and walked over to the garden where we could see the girl standing. The garden is surrounded by a metal fence, so we were on one side and the girl was on the other; we were only a couple of meters away so I could see the girl clearly this time. As I saw earlier, she was wearing a black dress and had long black hair to match. Her face had a deathly white pallor to it, but the most shocking attribute to the girl were her eyes. My wife had said they were dark, but seeing her close up, it was clear her eyes were jet black. No pupil, no iris, just pure blackness. There was no emotion on the girls face and she didn't move as we approached her; she just stared at us.

Now, I'm not stupid, I know you can get contact lenses which could explain what we were seeing, but there was just something a little strange about the girl and it seemed to invoke a certain degree of fear and terror in both of us. As my wife asked in a shaky voice whether she was on her own and needed help, the street lamps around us all shut off and everything was plunged into darkness. We could still see a little because of the ambient light around, but as we stared at the girl, it was like she was drawn backwards into the darkness and as soon as she was gone, the lights flicked back on. The garden was empty and there was no sign of the girl. We went in and searched with the help of torches on our mobile phones, but couldn't find anything out of the ordinary. It would have been impossible for her to have exited the gardens without us seeing and there's no logical explanation for what happened.

Over the next few weeks and months, we had regular sightings of the girl, both in the gardens opposite our house and also in the street. At first we tried to go out and speak to the girl but she would either be gone by the time we got there, or we would have the same strange situation with the lights shutting off. After a while we stopped trying because it was becoming just too scary.

We asked our neighbours if they had seen her or anything out of the ordinary, but they said they hadn't. However, I've since learned there are a couple of other stories in the area which involve people seeing a girl. One of them was near the railway bridge and in this case, someone had spoken to the girl and actually got a response. In that encounter the girl had said she was going to church, and then disappeared in front of the person. Apparently they had seen the girl again sometime later down our road, but I don't know whether this was in the gardens where we saw her.

Lenham Road, Headcorn
Alan T

I had been contacted by Louise, a lady who owned a house in Lenham Road in Headcorn. She reported to me that she regularly hears someone walking around in her living room late at night. When she comes to investigate, she can never find an explanation.

She also told me how small objects are moved around the room and placed in bizarre places. She was concerned that the incidents were starting to become more regular, and although she didn't feel in danger, she was still scared when she heard the noises.

In an effort to find a natural or logical explanation for the strange events, she asked if I would come to investigate. A colleague and I spent some time in different rooms of the house but didn't experience anything unusual and the noises she had reported weren't repeated.

I moved to the living room and set up a trail camera and two audio recorders in the room. This type of camera is typically used by wildlife enthusiasts; the self powered camera is normally attached to a tree and when it senses movement, a picture or video of the animal is taken. At the time, the camera I was using was motion sensitive, and took pictures using a flash in the same way as a normal camera. As with all technology, cameras available today are vastly superior to the one I was using and there are types of trail cameras where you can even stream live video to your mobile phone.

I sat with my colleague close to the only door in the room and waited. At 1:30 in the morning we heard a muffled noise coming from one of the corners of the room, opposite to where we were sitting. We waited and listened intently, when all of a sudden, we heard something fall over and the flash from the trail camera went off.

In the flash of light, we both saw a man standing in the corner of the room. He was elderly and dressed in clothes which would be considered from the 1970's. We both immediately stood up and turned on the ceiling light, however when we looked at where the man was standing, he had disappeared.

We checked the room for signs of entry (or possible exit) and the only thing out of place was a glass vase which had been knocked over. We checked the footage from the trail camera and there was no-one in the picture of the room. There is no explanation for this, as the camera had a perfect angle of where the man was standing. Discussing the event with my colleague, our descriptions matched and were both confident we had seen the same spirit.

Regent Way, Kings Hill

Jackie W

Kings Hill is a relatively new village on land which was previously RAF West Mailing. We moved into our home on the privately owned estate 18 months ago. It wasn't long after that we went to the local RSPCA and rescued an adult cat that had been poorly treated by her previous owner. We called her Sally after my daughter's favourite teddy bear which had gone missing the month before. It took some time, but she became a very loving and friendly cat, always wanting a cuddle or a stroke. Two months ago however, everything changed.

The problems started by her reacting to something she either saw or sensed upstairs. One day, I heard a growling noise coming from over by the stairs, so I looked over and saw Sally all puffed up and growling looking up the stairs, her tail was massive and her back was arched. She sank down and raised her hackles and when I went over to her, I could see her eyes were all "pupil", very much like how a cat's eyes dilate when they are hunting. It was very clear something had frightened her from up the stairs

This was the very first time I saw her appear "aggressive", she always has such a calm, sweet demeanour. So I could show my husband what she was like when he got home from work, I grabbed my phone, switched it to the video camera and began recording her at the bottom of the stairs. As I watched, she started to back up and then ran as fast as she could into the living room and hid behind the sofa.

When my husband returned that evening, I showed him the video. He pointed out what seemed to be an orb, a single, perfectly round white circle that floated down the stairs towards Sally, just as she ran away. Since that day, she won't come upstairs and sleep with us like she used to. We've tried carrying her up and putting her on the bed but as soon as we let her go, she immediately runs downstairs.

About two months after the incident on the stairs, I had gone to do the weekly shopping and my husband was at home with my daughter, who is 13. He was in the back garden clearing up the leaves which had dropped from the trees, and my daughter was upstairs getting ready to go to a party at a friend's house.

When I returned laden with the shopping, I came into the house to find my daughter downstairs in hysterics, with my husband trying to (unsuccessfully) calm her down. After a while and lots of cuddles and reassurances that everything would be OK, she finally told us what happened.

While she was getting ready she had just taken a shower and was drying herself in the bathroom. The mirror was fogged up and she had swiped her hand across it so she could see what her hair looked like. In the reflection, she could see an old man standing in the corner of the room, smiling at her.

She had spun around to look at who it was but there was no-one; the bathroom was empty apart from her. She told us that the wet towel which she'd pulled up to cover her front, was pulled away from her, leaving her naked. She'd screamed and ran into her room; my husband, hearing her cry, ran into the house thinking she'd hurt herself. He found her in her room quickly putting clothes on, after which he had taken her downstairs just before I arrived home.

Upon hearing the story of a man being in the bathroom with my daughter, I could see the anger in my husband's face as he ran upstairs and checked every possible place someone could be. No-one could be found and the front door had been locked when I got home. However, while we looked in the bathroom, the mirror had fogged up again and we could see that a word had been written in the condensation; all it said was "mine".

When things had calmed down, I sat with my daughter and talked to her about what she saw in the mirror. She explained that he was an elderly man, dirty and grubby looking with stubble around his face. She told us he had a horrible smile and his rotten teeth were on show. I tried to reassure my daughter that it must have been an illusion from the mirror and condensation in the room, but it was clear she was believed what she saw and was revolted by the thought that someone had seen her naked.

The thing is, I can't explain the word on the mirror and it wasn't written in any of our handwriting. I cleaned it that afternoon to make sure the word wouldn't reappear when someone else had a shower or bath. Later, my husband and I took my daughter out to the party but she was still shaken and I don't think she enjoyed it very much. From that point onwards, she has insisted on using our en-suite bathroom rather than the family bathroom, which, if it makes her feel better, I have no problems with.

There are other things which have happened since then which have caused concern for me. At night when she has gone to bed we sometimes hear her door close; my husband or I will go and check on her. We occasionally find her duvet pulled down and folded over neatly at the bottom of the bed and her pyjamas rearranged inappropriately. She's always fast asleep when we go in.

There have been a number of things go missing from her room. Nothing particularly sentimental or important, just things like a hairbrush, hair bands, socks and underwear or items like that. We found them completely by accident; they were in our attic over in a corner. The other thing we found was Sally, my daughters teddy bear, the one we had named the cat after. It must have been up there for months. Neither my husband or I put it up there and my daughter certainly couldn't have.

I'm a very down to earth person, not religious and I certainly didn't believe in the paranormal or supernatural. I've heard stories about how the area is haunted and some of the main buildings are meant to have ghosts, but I'd always laughed and dismissed them. However now I'm not so sure.

The Medway River, Larkfield
Daniel J

My grandad was in the army during the war, and I was fascinated by the stories he used to tell us about his exploits and the experiences he had. Growing up with tales of planes, tanks, ships and everything of that nature, I developed a huge interest in relics of the Second World War that still remain in the country and have visited many of them.

I have in the past visited many pill-boxes across Kent, but the vast majority of them are in bad condition, on private land, or have now been bricked up. However, I'd heard stories of a pill-box in pristine condition which was situated on the Medway river, close to New Hythe Station in Larkfield.

For those who don't know what a pill-box is, it's basically a guard post made of stone, brick or concrete. They have windows (called loopholes) for the soldiers to fire through. They were given the name "pill-box" because they have a similar hexagonal shape to that of the medicine pill containers which were sold at the time.

One day a friend and I decided to try to find the pill-box, so we took a drive and parked up at the station. We found the river easily enough and saw the entrance to the public footpath that runs alongside the river. At this point, we had a decision to make; do we turn right and walk towards Aylesford, or turn left towards Snodland? We tossed a coin and off to the left we walked, thinking we could always turn back if we don't find anything soon.

There had been a lot of rain recently and the river was high and flowing quickly, so we were glad we were on a concrete path rather than a country mud track! After a short walk, the industrial estate where the railway station is situated was left behind us and we started to walk into woods which were quite overgrown. The day was peaceful and all we could hear was the soft flowing of the river. As it turned out, our coin flipping was a success and off in the distance along the path we could see the concrete shape of the pill-box loom into view.

When we were nearing it, we could clearly see one of the windows of the pill box and although it was dark due to the overgrown trees causing a natural canopy, we saw someone staring straight at us. This person then moved back, away from the window. This was accompanied by the sound of heavy footsteps on the concrete floor of the pill box. We both slowed our walking, expecting someone to come out of the door, but no-one did. We continued along the path until we were stood outside the entrance.

We waiting for a while, not quite knowing what to do, until my friend called out "hello?". No response. We both repeated the call a couple of times, but yet there was no answer. Even though we were worried that it might be someone camped out inside (you always hear stories of drug users attacking people!) we both agreed we'd go in together. From the outside, the pill-box was the best we'd ever seen and there was no way we were leaving without at least taking a quick look inside!

We gingerly walked in, expecting someone to jump out at us, but that didn't happen. There was no one in there. Neither of us can explain what happened to the person; they definitely couldn't have left without us seeing them exit out the single door of the pill-box, and there wasn't anywhere inside for them to hide. It's a complete mystery! However, I would say, there was a huge difference in the temperature when we walked in; it was icy cold. I've often heard that is an indicator of the paranormal. Also, when we left and started walking back to the car, we both commented how it felt like we were about to get jumped on from behind, I know the hair on my neck was standing on end all the way back; I've never felt so frightened or paranoid!

Since then, I've learned there's a story associated with the nearby New Hythe Station where we had parked out car. The story tells of a ghost being seen on the platforms at night. I wonder if that has something to do with what we experienced?

St Peter and St Paul's Church, Leybourne

Susan B

Opposite the church there is a children's play area which I take my children to. I live quite nearby and on a nice sunny day, it's a great place to take them for a short walk. There's even a field with donkeys and horses and they love having an hour or so to play and say hello to the animals.

One sunny day, we went to the play park and while the children were having a great time on the equipment, I was leaning against the fence reading a book. We were the only people there so the children had the chance to run around and jump onto anything they wanted. Out of my peripheral vision, across the road I saw a man walk out of the wooden canopied entrance of the church, opposite to where I was standing. He stopped and stood still, so I looked up casually and saw something strange about him. He was dressed in some sort of historical garment and was stood pointing at me. I put my hand above my eyes to shield them from the bright sun, to see that the man had started to beckon me over by waving his hand; he pointed to the church and then walked back into the churchyard.

I wasn't sure what he wanted and not wanting to leave my children alone, I told them they needed to come with me to see the man in the churchyard. Based on the clothes the man was wearing, I made an assumption that the church was holding some sort of play or show and maybe he was inviting the children to see it?

We crossed the road and headed towards the church; I couldn't see the man any more. We started to walk under the canopy when I noticed the doors to the church were closed. Thinking it was odd the man would close the doors on us after beckoning us over, I told the children to stay under the canopy and I walked up to the church doors. As I had thought, they were shut and appeared locked.

It was at this point I started to feel strange; a little light headed and my legs went a bit wobbly. I started to walk back to the children, but it was like I was being drawn over into a different direction, further into the churchyard. I would describe it as being caught up in a current in the water. After a few moments, I walked around the corner of the chirch and saw the man further down the side, pointing at a place on the wall. As I drew nearer to him, he disappeared. When this happened, the strange feeling of being pulled in this direction disappeared too and I felt fine again. I know how ridiculous this all sounds, I'm usually a very level-headed person, but I can't describe it any other way.

I looked back and saw that my children had come into the churchyard and were watching me, so I told them I would be back in a moment. I didn't feel a need to leave, it was just the opposite. I felt as though I was where I was meant to be; it's a feeling that I find difficult to describe. Not wanting to keep my children waiting, we left and returned home.

A few days later when the children were at nursery, I went back to the church and had a longer look at the back of the church where the man was pointing. There was nothing unusual about it, so I walked round the front and into the church. I immediately spotted something on the opposite wall, which would have been exactly on the opposite side of where the man was pointing. I read the inscription and saw that it was the resting place of Sir Roger de Leybourne, someone who I had never heard of. I was suprised that someone would have the same name as the village, so I assumed he must have been an important person. There was another person in the church who I spoke to and they talked to me at length about the history of who Sir Roger was. It turns out he was the High Sheriff of Kent and went on a crusade to the Holy Land in 1271. Shortly after, he passed away while on the crusade, but I'm not sure of the cause.

Apparently in these circumstances the body of the deceased would be cut up and parts of the body such as the heart or brain would be encased in lead and sent back to their home country. In Sir Rogers case, it was his heart which was sent home and it was put into a double monument, with the intention that his wife would be buried there once she passed away. It was this monument that the man was pointing to from the other side of the during my previous visit.

During the Victorian age, the monument was opened and the two heart caskets were found; one had Sir Roger's heart but the other, which was intended for his wife, was empty. The man in the church told me that it was empty due to Lady de Leybourne remarrying after the death of her first husband. As a result, she was buried someone else once she died.

Like I said before, I'm a very level-headed person and I've previously never thought there were such things as ghosts. However, I truly believe I saw the ghost of Sir Roger de Leybourne that day. There is no other explanation I can give; it's not every day you are dragged towards a grave where you witness the figure of a man disappear right before your eyes! I can't explain why I didn't feel any terror and had the feelings I did when I experienced this, but I like to think it was the ghost of Sir Roger hoping that he wouldn't be alone any more. He hasn't appeared to me again, but I wonder if anyone else has experienced anything similar?

St Mary's Church Ruins, Little Chart
Megan H

My boyfriend Steve and I are really into all things spooky and scary. We've been on lots of ghost walks, stayed in haunted hotels and even paid to go on paranormal investigations with an events company. Unfortunately, we've never seen a ghost. That was until October last year.

For people in Kent who are interested in this sort of stuff, Pluckley is the pinnacle of places to go and visit. It has a huge reputation of being haunted and has been featured in the Guinness Book of World Records as being the most haunted village in Kent. Based on this, we decided to spend the day visiting the different haunted sites.

We found that a lot of them were in privately owned homes, so all we could do was take a quick glance and not linger about as it would look too suspicious! There was also a story about a haunted pub but that wasn't there anymore; it had been converted into houses. Apart from those, we had a great time; we even bumped into a group of other people who were doing the exact same thing as us! Unfortunately, we didn't see anything remotely paranormal.

We had a quick bite to eat in the Black Horse pub (another haunted location) and then headed out of Pluckley. The group we had spoken to earlier in the day had told us about another place that would be good to visit. It was a ruined church in Little Chart, not too far away and luckily for us, was on our way home.

When we arrived at what was left of the church, we found the tiny car park was empty. There was a huge sweeping drive that went around the back of the church but it was obviously a private drive so we avoided going anywhere near that. In the car park, there was an information board that gave details about what had happened to the church.

The church was apparently built by the Normans in the 11th century and had survived all those years until it was blown to pieces when it was hit by a doodlebug in the Second World War. Luckily, no-one had been killed or injured.

As we walked up the grassy bank towards the church ruins, we could see it towering above us. It was dusk, but everything was still clearly visible and we had no problems avoiding the graves and tomb stones. We walked up to the edge of the church and stepped over what used to be the wall. There were a few houses behind the church which we hadn't seen when we parked, so we tried to make sure anyone looking out of the windows wouldn't spot us. It's not like we were up to no good, we just didn't want the police to be called which apparently happens to would-be ghost hunters in Pluckley.

It seemed small for a church; we could see where the altar would have been, although nothing remained. The main architecture which was left standing was the tower area and the open archway of the door to the church. Just to the left of this, was a boarded-up door which we assumed would lead to the upper level of the tower. We could see the open door upstairs which should anyone come running through, they would just fall down to the ground floor again; a fall which would probably kill the person. It's no wonder it was boarded up. We tried to see if we could prise the wood boards off so we could go take a look upstairs, but it was solid and there was no movement at all. Whoever built this was a very good carpenter!

One of the pieces of information the group from earlier made us aware of, was that the altar was built facing the wrong way. Apparently they are meant to face a certain direction and this one didn't follow the correct template or pattern. For this reason, it is believed the church ruins are a prime location for something paranormal to happen. I don't know whether this is true, but the people from earlier were certainly convincing! We had a longer look around the back of the church and saw many overgrown but ornate graves.

On our way back to the car, we decided to go take a look at the tower again. We walked over to where the boarded-up door was, and almost immediately we both heard a scratching coming from behind it. It wasn't particularly loud to start with, but enough for us to hear. The scratching continued on the inside of the door, mixed with a few light knocks. Between the makeshift door and the wall, there was a very thin crack which we could look through. Steve peeked in but couldn't see anything because it was so dark. I gave him my phone which had a light on it and he tried again. This time, he took a look and turned to me and explained he could see the stone steps leading to the upstairs part of the church; he said they were covered in dust or sawdust or some other substance. He looked back into the crack to see what else could be seen.

As I was about to ask whether he could see what was making the noise, he gasped and looked at me with a huge grin on his face. He exclaimed, "I just saw a ghost! It's going up the stairs." We took a few steps back, so we could see the upper part of the tower and Steve pointed and said "Look!" Out of the open door at the top, we saw a white figure like shape come gliding out. I expected it to fall to the ground, but it didn't. It just glided out into the open above where we were standing and disappeared into the air.

Steve explained to me when he had looked back through the gap and had shone the light into the space, he had seen a man looking back at him. However, the man wasn't a solid person, his features weren't clear and seemed to be translucent. Steve said that the ghost had turned around and glided up the stairs. He went on to explain that he used the term glided because he couldn't see the legs moving, the lower part of the figure was "wispy and smoke like" if that makes sense at all. We've since suggested it looked a bit like a male version of the library ghost in Ghostbusters, without the horrible creature it turns into of course!

We waited around for a while to see if it came back, trying to look behind the boarded-up door many times, but nothing else appeared for us and there was no scratching heard either. We did note that whatever the dust was on the stairs, it hadn't been disturbed at all by the ghost travelling up the stairs. After a while we headed back to the car, took a final look at the tower just in case the ghost was there again (it wasn't of course!) and headed home. All in all, it was a fantastic day, rounded off with us seeing our very first ghost!

Main Road, Longfield
Steve A

A few years ago, I took my children (one boy aged 11 and a girl aged 8) to a boot fair near to where Brands Hatch race course is located. It was huge and one of the largest I've ever been to. Those of you who frequent boot fairs will know the majority of items people sell are absolute rubbish; basically what they couldn't sell on Ebay. However, my kids love going to them and usually end up getting some toys or things to play with. I like them because I spend very little money in comparison to going to a toy shop!

On this day, I was looking at a stall with books and my children had wandered a little further to the next few tables. While I was picking through the many books, my son came running over to me with something in a bag. He was very excited and extremely pleased with himself. When he got to me, he immediately opened the bag to show me the contents and shouted, "Look what I've got!" I looked in and thought it was hilarious, all be it hideous at the same time; it was an old ventriloquist dummy.

I looked at the face staring up at me for a few seconds before I remembered that I hadn't given my children any money yet, so I asked him how he'd paid for the dummy. My son told me the man a few stalls down the row said he could have it for free. I did believe my son as he's a very honest person, but I said we should go over to the stall where he got it from; just to make sure the owner was happy with his decision and to thank him for the free gift.

When we got to the stall, the man was hurriedly packing up and practically throwing his other items back into his car. When he saw my son and the bag, he looked worried. Thinking he was worried I was going to make a complaint or something like that, I reassured him we were grateful for the free gift, but I wanted to check whether he wanted some money for the item. It was quite large and must have been worth something so giving it away for free was very generous. Cutting me off before I finished my sentence, he adamantly told me that my son was to keep the dummy. His demeanour changed and he developed a wild, crazed look in his eyes. His stance became more aggressive and insisted that the dummy had chosen my son, it was now his. With that he returned to packing his car up.

Believing he was either eccentric or insane, I took my son's hand and we went and found my daughter who had found a stall with a box of teddy bears and was busy deciding which one she should take home. My son thrust the bag under her nose to show her his prized possession (I'm sure he knew it would terrify her!) and she recoiled in horror, my son giggling at the response. I pulled him away, helped her choose her teddy bear and we headed home to give my wife the good news about the free gift.

At home, we found my wife and my son took the dummy out of the bag to show her. Let's just say, she wasn't particularly impressed! Now it was out of the bag, we could see the state it was in. It had been extensively repaired with masking tape and it was in a very sorry state. The jaw, which would normally open and close was stuck fast, it looked as though it had been glued shut and as much as I tried, I couldn't prise it open. It had no clothes so it was basically a head with hair that was greasy and matted down, a stuffed body covered in tape and little black plastic boots stuck to the end of the legs. All in all, it was a mess, but my son loved it and for about six weeks he took it everywhere with him, talking to it and pretending to listen to what the dummy was saying. He called it 'Tapey' because of all the masking tape keeping it together.

One day, I came into the living room and saw my son sat on the sofa, staring into space. Tapey, his usual companion was nowhere to be seen. I asked if he was OK and he told me he didn't like Tapey and they weren't friends any more I sat down and asked what had happened. My son said that Tapey had started to say bad things, was scaring him and was keeping him awake at night. Assuming this was a child's overactive imagination, I played along with him as he was obviously upset about the situation. I told him we could put Tapey in a box and put him in the attic or out in the garage. When I said this, we heard a loud crash come from upstairs. I went up to see what had caused it, only to find my son's TV screen had been broken. There was a huge crack across the screen with a small hole in the middle where something had obviously hit it. I looked around the floor and found a marble; it's the only thing which was around that could have damaged the screen and the hole matched the size of the marble. As always, the dummy was sat on my son's bed.

When I told my son what had broken, he was obviously upset and immediately blamed the dummy. He told me how he'd put the dummy in the cupboard under the stairs and had gone to sit in the living room. In my mind, for the dummy to get back up onto his bed, the only explanations were that my son was confused about putting the dummy in the cupboard, someone else had moved it back upstairs, or unbelievably, the dummy had made it up to the bedroom on its own. As my son and I were the only people in the house I'm sure you can guess what I thought, but as he was upset about the TV, I didn't push the matter. I also couldn't explain how the TV had been smashed with the marble as it happened when we were both downstairs in the living room. As promised, I took the dummy away, put it in a box and left it in our garage.

This is when the unexplained things started to happen, and believe me, I know only too well how implausible and farfetched they sound!

At night, when the kids were in bed, my wife and I would hear the patter of feet upstairs. When we would go and check on the children, they would be fast asleep. Objects would either be moved or disappear completely, only to turn up in the most bizarre places. My wife would hear giggling and other noises in the house when the children were at school.

One Sunday, I had taken the children swimming and my wife was cleaning my son's room; as she was hoovering around his bed, she had a fright. She had looked under his bed ready to push the end of the hoover under, when she had seen two eyes staring back at her. It was Tapey. When she recovered from the shock, she grabbed him, took him downstairs and threw him into the cupboard under the stairs.

When we returned from the swimming pool, she asked him why he'd taken Tapey out of the garage. He replied he hadn't, Tapey had done it by himself. I went to the cupboard to get the dummy, but couldn't see where my wife had put him. I called her over and we both looked; with an increasingly sinking feeling, we decided the dummy wasn't in the cupboard any more. I could tell by the look on my wife's face that we both knew where we needed to look next.

My wife and I went up to my son's room and walked to the bed. I knew neither of us wanted to look, but knew we had to. I got down on all fours and looked under the bed and as expected, saw two eyes glaring back at me. My stomach just dropped. Although I didn't want to touch it, I grabbed the doll and we went downstairs. When my children saw it, they both burst into tears. While my wife consoled them, I took the dummy outside and put it in the bin, thinking that would be the end of it. It wasn't.

The following day I went to put some rubbish in the bin; when I opened the lid, the dummy was gone. I went straight back upstairs and looked under my son's bed. Thankfully, there was nothing under it. Relieved, I stood up and turned around only to see Tapey sat on the shelf behind the door; his eyes staring blankly at me and his grin as menacing as always. I grabbed the dummy and went to the garden; I grabbed a spade which was next to the garage and smashed the dummy's head into pieces. I have to say, I thoroughly enjoyed that part! I also used the spade to separate the body, tearing open the masking tape. Dirty stuffing came spilling out together with a small leather bag. I opened the bag and inside I found a powder of some sort, what looked like dried herbs and what I believe was a couple of small animal bones.

I dug a deep hole and placed the smashed remains of the dummy, the stuffing and the bag at the bottom. From the garage I grabbed some fire-lighters and liquid which we use to light our barbecue and set light to the evil thing at the bottom of the hole. As the flames engulfed the tangled mess of smashed and torn dummy, I felt a huge sense of relief. When the flames were out, I covered the hole with soil and stamped it down. As far as my wife and children are concerned, the final part of the story never happened and they think the dummy was taken away by the dustmen. I have no plans to tell them Tapey's remains are buried in the garden!

Tonbridge Road, Maidstone
Sarah V

When I was growing up, we lived in a terraced home and the basement had been converted into my bedroom. The first time something strange happened I was about 14 years old and was in my room, reading a book on my bed. I heard the front door open and close, then heard someone walking across the living room into the dining room. The stairs down to my bedroom were situated in the corner of the living room, and this is where I heard the footsteps stop.

I assumed it was one of my parents returning from work, but being in the house on my own and at the age I was, I became nervous as it seemed the person was just standing at the top of my stairs. I called out, "Hello mum? Dad?" to see if they would answer, but no response came. I called out again but there was still nothing, so I pushed my head around the corner and looked up to the top of the stairs. No-one was there.

I went upstairs and checked the rest of the house but I was alone. I had no explanation for what I heard and my parents also confirmed they hadn't been home earlier when I questioned them.

The next day, the same thing happened when I was in my room and I was the only person in the house. Again, I couldn't find an explanation.

This happened on a regular basis while I was growing up; nothing negative ever happened and I don't believe the spirit was malevolent at all. I would just hear the sounds of the door opening and then footsteps. No-one else ever heard them while they were on their own and in their respective rooms.

When I was older, about 25, I bought a place of my own and moved out. My parents turned my old bedroom in the basement into a craft room for my mum where she could go to be creative and relax.

I was visiting her one Sunday afternoon, when she suddenly turned to me and asked if I had ever heard the ghost. I asked what she was talking about, and she explained how sometimes when she is in her craft room (my old bedroom) with her mind engrossed in her knitting or crochet she has regularly experienced something strange. We went on to describe how she hears the front door open, then there are footsteps of someone walking across the living room into the dining room and stop at the top of the stairs. When she checks, there is never anyone there.

Tonbridge Road, Maidstone
Chris B

A few years ago, we bought a house in Maidstone which needed a lot of work doing to it. Nothing structural, mostly cosmetic work like decorating, replacing some of the doors and other work of that nature. However, we needed to also have a new boiler put in, have the electrics replaced and some of the pipework repaired.

The house was laid over three floors and had a room under ground level. I suppose most people would call it a basement or cellar, but as it had been converted properly into a room, we didn't see it like that. One of the previous owners had grills put into the floors to allow the air to circulate around the house. These also needed removing as part of the boiler and pipe replacement.

We had lived in the house for a couple of months while deciding what work to do first and saving some money; it was going to cost quite a lot to do everything we needed! When I say 'we', I mean my wife and my baby girl, who was six months old. When the work was about to begin, my wife and daughter moved into her parents due to the amount of dust the building work was going to generate.

While removing the air flow grills in my daughter's bedroom, one of the builders found a number of items which had been put between the floors. Most were little trinkets like a brooch and some old coins, but there was also a pair of little baby shoes. They looked really old. The builders threw the shoes away and some of the other items that looked worthless, but the items that looked like they may be worth something were kept to get valued later on.

That night when the builders had packed away and gone home, I was working in my study on the computer. In this room I have a baby monitor which is connected to the one in my daughter's room. Having listened to the hiss from the monitor for six months now, I find the noise of silence quite soothing so I had it on in the background while I was concentrating on my work.

After a while, I heard the noise of movement coming from the monitor. Confused, as I was alone in the house, I turned the monitor up so I could hear better, still thinking I had misheard. I knew it wasn't my imagination when I heard a young child, a boy, say, "where are my shoes; I can't find my shoes", and then there was a huge crash.

I rushed upstairs to my daughter's bedroom and threw open the door; as you are probably expecting, there was no child there. However all the builders' tools were strewn across the floor. I was shocked. If it was just the voice I'd heard, I could maybe put it down to interference on the baby monitor, or that it had picked up another radio transmission and it was just a co-incidence we had removed the shoes earlier that day (a huge coincidence, I know). But with the tools being thrown around the room, I knew that wasn't the case and there was a more paranormal explanation.

I went outside to the bin, grabbed the shoes and other items which had been thrown away earlier, and put them back into the room. I tidied up the tools, closed the door and went back to my study to listen to the baby monitor.

About ten minutes later, I heard movement, then a child giggled and then all was silent. I raced back to the room, and it was just as I had left it. I spent the rest of the night listening to the baby monitor, but didn't hear anything else.

When the builders returned, I made them put all the items back where they had found them and they were sealed back up. I haven't had anything else happen in the house since!

Oakwood Hospital / Maidstone Hospital (Psychiatric Wing), Maidstone

Kate S

I worked at the hospital for many years before its closure. But back when I started, I had a strange experience working the night shift. As a little bit of background, the hospital was originally called "Kent County Lunatic Asylum" and started operating in 1833.

I was in the office with a colleague and we were having a chat. It was nothing in particular and I don't really remember what the subject was so it can't have been important. We had the door open and we could see down the corridor. Out of the corner of my eye I saw movement, so I looked over.

There was a man standing where the corridor joined another, basically at a cross junction in the hallway. Although he was a way off, I could see he had a confused look on his face. Although we had many patients, he didn't look familiar and there was something just a little strange about him. The clothes he was wearing were certainly not the type which belonged to the hospital, although they did have the appearance of a hospital garment.

In my peripheral vision, he appeared solid, but when I looked directly at him, he wasn't. He seemed hazy or fuzzy, like when you see someone standing in the mist. Its difficult to describe, but it all made me feel a little strange, as if the energy of the place was out of sync.

I wasn't sure if it was because it was late and I was tired, or the long shifts had gotten to me. I blinked a few times, looked away and then looked back, but he was still there, looking confused. He definitely wasn't a solid figure.

I stood up to go and find out what was going on, but the man took a step back and disappeared. It was like he just vanished as if he had never been there in the first place. I asked my colleague whether he had seen the man; he looked into the corridor and told me he hadn't, but he later told me that he sees things in the corridors all the time which can't be explained. He seemed relieved I had seen something too, I think he was afraid he'd end up as one of the patients!

When I asked other staff about this, they explained that in the 1950's, a fire had started in the tailors workshop and a number of people had been injured and some had even died. I was told firemen, nurses and a patient died when a tower collapsed on them. It was believed by some of the staff that their spirits were still in the hospital. Although I had only seen one, other nurses had seen other strange things in different areas of the hospital as well that they can't explain.

The hospital has now been converted into flats; I wonder if any of the residents have experienced anything unusual?

Victoria Road, Margate
Mark L

I was 16 when this happened, my friend and I were doing our GCSEs and the way in which our exams were scheduled, it meant we had an afternoon off, which was something of a rarity for us!

We had returned home to my house and as my parents were still at work, we were alone in the house. This was in the days before the internet and we had become bored very quickly and were looking for something to do. My friend had an idea and suggested that we make a Ouija board and have some fun.

We found a candle and a short glass in the cupboard, turned off all the lights, pulled the curtains and in the dim light of the single flickering flame, made our own board by writing letters onto an A4 piece of blank paper. We finished it off with a 'yes' and `no' in the top corners and a 'goodbye' at the bottom in the middle. We stuck the home-made board to the table with some sellotape. We were proud of our creation!

My friend started asking questions like "is there anyone there?" as we moved the upturned glass around the board. We continued like this for a while and on the whole, nothing really happened apart from some resistance to pushing the glass around. I assumed this was my friend trying to spook me, but she was adamant it wasn't her.

We were about to give up when my friend asked for a spirit to show us a sign that there was anyone with us. When she did this, the atmosphere seemed to change and I had what I'd describe as a ringing in my ears. The flame on the candle started to become larger, then smaller and repeated again and again, making it look like it had a heartbeat.

My friend and I looked at each other, eyes and mouths wide open, when the flame was suddenly extinguished, plunging the room into darkness. We both screamed and I ran to put the light on. As the light filled the room, I could see my friend still sat at the table, looking panicked. I went back and sat with her, trying to calm her down. As she looked up and around the room, she spotted something on the ceiling and cried out in fear. Directly above where the candle had been, there was a dark shape caused by what I assumed was the soot from the flame and wick. It was the perfect silhouette of a face, with menacing eyes and a mouth wide with a sneer.

I initially thought was just a coincidence and that it was caused by the smoke of the candle on the uneven surface of the ceiling. That was until the eyes closed, followed by a loud snap as a crack appeared across the face and continued across the ceiling. My friend and I bolted out of the house. As we leaped out of the front door we both heard a crash behind us.

We ran to my friend's house and called my parents; they arrived soon after and took me home. As we entered the room where we were having our Ouija board session, we saw part of the ceiling had come down, smashing the table with the heavy plaster. I'm glad we had made our escape when we did.

My dad said it was because the house was old and the ceiling needed replacing, but I'm not so sure. After that, I hated living there; I was terrified all the time and was constantly expecting something else to happen. As soon as I got a job, I moved straight out.

Maidstone Road, Matfield
Steph T

This happened a few years ago near to where I live, when I was driving towards the village of Matfield from the direction of the A21.

Just as you enter the village, on the right there is an old, small cemetery where some (but not all) of the graves have been moved because of the building of houses. I believe they were moved up to the church on the outskirts of the village, but I may be wrong on that. It was mid-afternoon on a summer's day.

As I was coming up to the cemetery, I glanced over and saw a man and a child planting flowers on a grave just by the fence and gate, nearest the road. I could clearly see the people; the man was wearing a dark grey suit and his hair was slicked back. I remember thinking how it was the same style my grandad used to have when he was younger. The little girl was facing the road and was wearing an old style dress with a hat; I could see her blonde curls coming out from under the hat.

As I passed, I slowed down to look at the man planting the flowers; I could see him using a gardening tool to dig some of the earth away. My gaze then fell onto the girl who was looking directly at me, who then raised her arms up and held them out like children do when they want to be picked up. I'll never forget the look on her face, she had a look of pure loneliness and longing.

My gaze went back to the road; I couldn't shake the feeling of how completely out of place they looked, and I have to admit, I was distressed at the look the girl had given me. I pulled over at the village pub, the Wheelwrights, got out of my car and started to walk back to the cemetery, crossing the road.

Looking at the cemetery, which is about 100 yards up the road, I couldn't see either the man or the girl. As I arrived at the cemetery gate a few short moments later, my suspicions were confirmed and they were gone. They certainly couldn't have walked out of the cemetery and up the road as I'd be able to see them (it's a long straight road), so I assumed they must have gone to the back of the cemetery, which is behind a large tree.

I looked at the grave where the man had been digging a spot for the flowers he was holding, but the grass which covered the entire cemetery was undisturbed and there were no flowers either. I opened the metal gate which made a loud squeaking sound as it moved and stepped into the cemetery. Even though it was a nice, warm summer's afternoon, it was like I had stepped into a chiller cabinet. I was shocked at the sudden change in temperature, so I hurried towards the back and made my way around the tree, calling out "hello?" as I went.

There was no one there and also no way for anyone to leave the cemetery without me seeing; like I say it is very small, only about 100 yards in length and 10 in width. By this point, I was spooked, so I hurried back to my car and left the coldness behind.

I've since learned that the pub I stopped my car at is also meant to be haunted. After that experience, each time I drive through the village and past the old cemetery, I never look over into it any more. I always get the feeling I'll see the girl and the man again!

The Forgotten Gate, Park Road, Mereworth
Tom G

A few years ago I was with my dad and we both saw a ghost. Between Mereworth and Wateringbury, there is a country lane that links two main roads. The country lane goes past St Michael's Church which is also meant to be haunted, although I've never seen anything there. Along this road, there is a sharp corner which has a huge ornate, but derelict stone gate set back from the road. It's enormous and is on the private property of Mereworth Castle. It's not possible to go through it, there is no path or lane and its all fenced off and overgrown.

Mereworth Castle is very old and goes back hundreds of years. I think the current house was built in about 1700 and is a listed building. Unfortunately, you can't go into the castle as it's privately owned.

The country lane leads around the gate and has quite a wide corner where you can park. My dad used to park here and walk our dog in the fields. I would sometimes go with him and it was on one of our walks that we saw something supernatural.

We had parked up in the space at the corner and were getting out of the car when we heard what sounded like a whip crack. It's not often you hear something like that so we weren't sure what it was. We looked around and couldn't see anything, there were no other cars or people around and by now everything was quiet (it's quite an isolated location in the country). We carried on and got the dog out the back of the car and went for our walk.

About an hour later, we had just got back to where the car was parked and we heard another loud crack, but this time it was followed by the sounds of horse hooves. It sounded like it was coming from over in the direction of the old gate so we looked over to see what it was. I didn't think any horse could possibly be galloping that fast based on the sounds I was hearing, especially as the area around the gate is wooded and so overgrown.

My dad and I were asking each other what we thought it could be, when a horse came galloping out of the gate with a man riding it directly towards where we were standing. What made this a totally bizarre experience, was that the horse and man, although appearing solid, were racing through all the foliage and they also came directly through, not over, the fence. As they came across the road, the sounds of the hooves didn't change either, they sounded as though they were still on packed earth rather than the road surface.

My dad grabbed me by my collar and pulled me away from the car just as the man and the horse went through it, making the car rock slightly. They then went through the hedge and trees behind us and disappeared; the sounds of the hooves stopping abruptly. My dad and I went back into the field but we couldn't see them anywhere. We were both a little shaken but to ease the tension, my dad said, "That must have been the ghostly highway man".

It turns out in West Peckham, a short distance away, there are stories about a highwayman called Jack Diamond who haunts a house which he apparently used to live in. I've always assumed ghosts of highwaymen would wear the stereotypical garb you see on the telly with the hat and the long black coat, but our phantom highwayman didn't wear any of that. He was in a brown leather coat and a pair of loose black trousers with brown boots. No hat was worn, but on the horse were a couple of saddlebags and a whip poking out. Thinking about it, none of the clothes he wore were like what you'd expect a horse rider to wear today, they seemed to be in keeping with something you'd expect to see in the age of highwaymen. The stories about Jack Diamond say his ghost appears on Friday the 13th at the West Peckham house, but this was a Saturday in late July, so maybe this could be the location he haunts the rest of the year?

Lossenham Lane, Newenden
Bethany C

My family has always had experiences with the paranormal; each of us have witnessed or been the focus of something unusual and strange. My parents and sister moved around a lot when I was younger because of my dad's job, so we rented rather than owned our own home. It seemed that no matter where we lived, there would be some type of haunting there. Sometimes it would take a while for whatever it was to start happening, but eventually whatever it was, it would make an appearance.

We had been living on the border of Kent for a while, in the village of Newenden when we were advised our landlord needed to sell the house. He was in a financial crisis and urgently needed the money. As we had a good relationship with him, he gave us first refusal on the property. At this point, nothing paranormal had happened in the house and as the deal was so good due to the landlords situation, my parents snapped up the house. This was the first time I lived in a home we owned outright and for some strange reason, it felt so much more like a home after the ownership had changed.

Everything went well for months, there was nothing untoward and things were happy in the family. We thought we'd put the whole paranormal thing behind us, then about five months after living there, things started to happen and the whole atmosphere of the house changed. It started off really small, with items such as keys going missing, or sometimes the TV or our Sky box would just turn on and off by itself. Generally the type of thing that can be easily explained away, but with our history, the subject of a haunt would linger at the back of our minds. After another couple of months of items moving, disappearing or electrical problems, the activity started to slowly increase.

Chairs started to move by themselves, doors would open and close on their own, that sort of deal. These were things that had happened to us in the past in previous houses, so it wasn't that much of a concern to any of us. We initially just put it down to just another house being haunted. However, the activity continued to get worse and worse and it was focussed mostly on me, which is something that wouldn't normally happen.

I would be woken up in the middle of the night and hear voices coming from the living room. It was the sort of thing where you'd be upstairs and hear the television on downstairs; it was just noise in the background. It would be loud enough for me to hear all the way upstairs behind my shut door and be clear enough for me to hear what was actually being said. I'd get up, open my door and look down the stairs and all the lights would be off and the house would be silent and dark. My parents and sister would be fast asleep in their own rooms and normally if a television was actually on, there would be some sort of light coming up from the living room, so it clearly wasn't the case in this instance.

After a while I'd start waking up to other types of noises as well; I'd hear scratching on the inside of my bedroom walls and the doors to my wardrobe would rattle or open on their own. I'd also be able to hear the scratching coming from inside the wardrobe as well. I know a lot of people would say it could've been a rat or a mouse in the wall or in my room, but I know it wasn't; the scratches were long and drawn out, like someone pulling their fingernails all the way down the wall. Sometimes it would keep me awake for so long, I'd have to leave the room and sleep somewhere else.

One week I was away on a school trip to an activity centre and I stayed there for five nights. When I came home, my mum told me how she'd been woken up by noises in my room and when she'd checked, there was nothing there. She went on to tell me how she'd also heard what sounded like two men talking in my room but can't explain where the voices had come from. Each day while I was away, she'd come into my room and found my wardrobe doors wide open. In the end she'd tied them together with some string, only to return later and find them open again and the string snapped and on the floor.

These things continued to happen even after I left for university. Although my room is bigger than hers, my sister refused to have it and my parents turned my room into what was effectively a storage room. They tell me sometimes how they can hear movement within the room and sometimes the heavy boxes are either repositioned or knocked over!

Brookers Oast, The Hop Farm, Paddock Wood
Shane W

It was an evening in late November when I was due to meet a group of my friends at the pub at the Hop Farm. At the time I would have called myself a sceptic, I blatantly didn't believe in the paranormal and certainly wouldn't have considered tha there are such things as ghosts. However, after this experience, there is no question in my mind that such things do exist.

It was dark when I arrived at the pub and thankfully the rain had stopped. As I pulled into the driveway and car park of the pub, I saw some of my friends standing outside. They weren't waiting for me to arrive, they are smokers and were having their fix of nicotine. I wound the window down and we said our hellos. One of them pointed out to the car park and said "There's a space over there, you two can park there." I was a little confused as I was on my own, I just said "uh OK" and drove over to the space and reversed in.

I locked the car and walked over to my friends. We exchanged pleasantries and made a little small talk when one of my friends asked, "Isn't she coming to join us?" All my friends turned to me and again I was confused. I asked, "Who?" He responded, "The girl you came with, are you going to keep her locked in the car all night?" I laughed, thinking they were winding me up, when another friend, said, "No, seriously, who is she? Why don't you want to introduce her?" I said, "Stop messing around, I'm on my own." My friend responded, "So who is that in your car?"

We looked over and to my amazement, there was a woman sat in my car. She must have been in her mid-twenties and quite pretty; she was sat in the passenger seat looking straight over at us. I said, "How did she get in my car?" to which my friend answered, "You drove in with her". My heart stopped and my stomach dropped. I tried to tell my friends that I was on my own but they wouldn't believe me.

I persuaded them to come over to the car with me and as we approached, right before our eyes the girl disappeared. We all jumped a mile; one of my friends ran into the pub in fright (he's never lived that down!). We looked in the windows of the car but there was no-one there and the doors were still locked.

Bewildered, we went into the pub, found the rest of our friends and told them about the experience. None of them believed us, but we know what we saw. I have no idea how long she had been in the car or where she went. I makes me wonder whether sometimes other ghosts hitch a ride without being seen!

Smarden Road, Pluckley
William H

A few weeks ago, my wife and I had a strange experience. We live in a rural village, Pluckley, which is well known for having a plethora of ghosts. I don't put much stock in those stories; I think they were mostly made up to try to bring people and tourists to the businesses here. We have two children, aged four and six, who have their own bedrooms just down the corridor to ours.

It was just before midnight and everyone in the house apart from me was asleep. I know this because I'd recently done my nightly check on my children which I do every night just before going to bed. I was just dropping off to sleep myself when all of a sudden I awoke to the noise of tiny feet pattering down the corridor outside my room.

I immediately got up to assist whichever of my children it was, concerned that it was out of character for them to be running round the house in the dark. If they need the toilet, they would normally call me or my wife to put the lights on before they get out of bed.

To my shock, there was no-one in the corridor or in the bathroom and the house was dark and still. Thinking they may have gone to their rooms when they heard me getting up, I checked only to find them both asleep, in the same positions I had recently left them. Puzzled, I returned to bed thinking I must have imagined it as I was half asleep when I had heard the noise.

As I got into bed, my wife rolled over and asked who was running round the house. It was then that we both heard a child giggling and it sounded like it was coming from the corner of our bedroom. Startled, I threw myself out of bed and ran to the light switch. My wife shrieked and sat bolt upright in bed. The light came on and thankfully the room was empty apart from us.

However, my wife, who was now clearly terrified and shaking, explained that as she had heard the laughter, she had looked over in the darkness. She said she saw two eyes looking back at her from the corner of the room but as soon as the light came on, they disappeared. We have no explanation for what my wife saw, but we both feel very uncomfortable in the house now. If it wasn't for the financial issues of moving, we would sell up and move away.

The Black Horse, Pluckley
Alan T

This pub dates back to the 1470's when it was a farmhouse to the Dering family. It is well known for its ghosts and has featured on several paranormal television shows. Allegedly one of the ghosts regularly moves the glasses and possessions of the staff and customers. Many people have also reported the ghost of a child in the pub.

My story dates back to when I was first investigating the paranormal. Pluckley is usually high on the list for many people who want to start ghost hunting. The inevitable trek through the screaming woods, a visit to the church cemetery and the other known haunts will inevitably be an enjoyable experience. Unless of course you try to do it around Halloween which is when some friends and I decided to; it wasn't long before we were moved on by the police, who increase their patrols around that time of year.

Due to this and the lack of ghosts wanting to meet us that night, we returned to The Black Horse where we had started the evening. We had arrived and parked in the gravel car park which is behind the pub. Even though it was October and was quite cold outside, the car full of people had soon become too warm so we all had our windows open.

We were all sat in the car, talking about the nights events (or lack of them), when one of my friends asked, "do you hear that?" We all became deathly silent and listened. Initially nothing happened, but then we heard footsteps on the gravel outside the car. They became quite loud, as if someone was walking towards us; but there was no one there. The sound of the footsteps crunching on the gravel stopped outside the passenger door for a moment, then started walking around the car, round and round.

We all looked out of our windows, not quite believing it was what we thought it was. I could see indentations in the gravel where someone had walked, when a friend shouted, "look at the window!"

We all turned our attention to the windscreen to see a small hand print appear and the sound of a little girl giggle. We all jumped out of the car and looked all around but couldn't find anyone.

I've been back to the pub and car park several times to see if the girl would revisit, but never had anything else happen.

Ransley Green, Ruckinge
Jen G

When I was a teenager, my parents split up and I lived with my mother. I had two sisters and a brother who also lived with me.

My mother was really into the occult and had managed to get a Ouija board. Back in those days it was hard unless you made one yourself as you couldn't buy them in the shops. Once she had it in her hands, she was like a woman possessed. She was completely obsessed with it and there were many evenings where we had to fend for ourselves and make our own food and put the younger children to bed. She mostly used it in her bedroom, away from us. I suppose you could say the environment of the house was not a positive one at that time. I don't know if this is linked to my experience but I thought I should mention it.

One night when I was 17, I walked into my bedroom and was about to go to bed. I always had a feeling like a presence was in that room watching me, and that particular night the feeling was very strong. I switched the light off and ran to my bed and laid down, hoping I'd get to sleep quickly.

Shortly after I had gotten into the bed, the room was pitch-black and I couldn't see a thing. I started to get a strange feeling and I sensed that there was a presence right next to my bed. Whatever it was seemed to be right next to me and I could feel its gaze burning into my face. I got the feeling it had an evil intent and meant me harm. I was completely terrified and wanted to hide myself under the covers like a child but for some reason I couldn't force myself to turn away, it was like I was frozen in fear. I can't describe the terrible feeling I felt, I was convinced whatever this was, even though I couldn't see anything, was evil.

I managed to pull my gaze away from the darkness of the room and rolled over onto my back. Suddenly I couldn't move, my body was paralysed. I couldn't speak or cry for help even though I wanted to scream.

I know some people will say this was sleep paralysis, but I wasn't asleep and had only just gotten into bed. I hadn't even closed my eyes.

I felt a pressure bearing down on me from above, it was literally pushing me into the mattress of the bed. I could feel heat against my face but still couldn't see what it was in the room. Everything was pitch black, darker than it had ever been in the room. I was terrified, but all of a sudden, the pressure lifted and the darkness seemed to clear. Although the room was still dark, it wasn't anything like it was just a few moments before.

The strange thing was, I didn't get up and run out of the room. I just lay there, still frightened and dropped off to sleep. In any situation like this, I would be the first person to say to run and get out of the room or house, so I can't understand why I just stayed there and went to sleep.

Meadow Road, Rusthall
Joshua T

This story relates to an encounter in one of the bay windowed Victorian houses on Meadow Road. I've later learned there have been rumours of paranormal activity in these houses for some time.

When my wife and I first came to view the property, it immediately felt like home. It had a warm, inviting feel about it so we immediately put in an offer and it was accepted. The first year living here was wonderful and we were very happy. However the house needed quite a bit of modernising so we had to make changes slowly.

One of the things we liked the most about the house was the wealth of original features, such as the old in built cabinets and the cast iron fireplaces. We knew these had to be kept to help keep the value of the property. Over time we made many changes, particularly in the upstairs back room which we converted into a bathroom. In this room we had to remove one of the fireplaces as some work needed to be done on the chimney stack. We kept the fireplace in the shed in the back garden, hoping to sell it later.

Shortly after this building work was completed, we started to hear noises coming from the room which was now the bathroom. We thought they sounded like creaking and knocking, which we initially put down to the sounds of the house settling at night. However, the sounds increased in volume over time and we were even convinced one night we heard the sound of someone walking across the stripped pine floor boards in the room.

One day, I was in our dining room downstairs having my lunch at the dining table when out of the corner of my eye I saw something move in the corner of the room. I stood up and witnessed the shape of a person walk from one side of the room to the other, ending up going through the open door to the cupboard under the stairs. To say I was terrified is an understatement, but I knew I had to pluck up the courage and look under the stairs to find out what happened to it. I crept over to the cupboard and peeked inside, but there was nothing there.

I've often found it difficult to explain what the thing looked like; I initially thought it was a shadow, but it wasn't on the wall like a normal shadow; it was a 3D shape and was in the room with me, like person made of static.

When I told my wife what I'd seen, she admitted that when she was takes a bath, she sometimes thinks she sees movement out of the corner of her eye too, but could never explain what it was. She explained it just felt like someone was there.

The strange thing about all this is that a few weeks later we were going to put the fireplace on the internet to sell, so I went to the shed to take pictures. When I opened the shed door, I was pushed back by an unknown force; I literally knocked me off my feet. When I stood up and looked in the shed, I saw that the fireplace had been completely smashed to pieces. I have no idea whether all these things are connected or what actually happened to the fireplace. It was made out of cast iron after all, it seems impossible that something so strong can suddenly be broken into pieces. Since then, the noises have continued in the bathroom, but thankfully neither of us have ever witnessed the shadow person again.

Springfield Road, Sittingbourne
Dorothy U

I used to live on my own in a lovely house in one of the quiet and tranquil streets of Sittingbourne. However, eventually I felt there was no other alternative but to move out after living here for many years. This was all because of the increasing paranormal activity which was taking place.

It had started innocently enough, with personal items such as a watch or keys going missing. Initially I thought they had just been misplaced, but after some time they would appear in the most bizarre places, such as in the spare bedroom or even dropping down from the chimney. It was the recovery of the items that made me believe it certainly wasn't me misplacing the items, especially in the case of the chimney incident!

On several occasions, noises could be heard throughout the house, not just by me, but also my friends. These seemed to sound like whispers, but no-one could ever make out what was being said, or where it was coming from. This spooked my friends so much, several of them refused to enter my home, saying it felt as though someone was whispering in their ears.

Although unnerved, I remained strong and resolute that there was a logical explanation for what was happening, but a chance encounter with one of my neighbours across the road changed my mind on the subject.

While doing some gardening, my neighbour, whom I had known for several years, approached me and asked who the gentleman was that I was dating. A little perplexed at the question, I replied I wasn't seeing anyone and wondered why my neighbour had asked this out of the blue.

My neighbour explained as she lives directly across the road, she can see into some of the windows, even at night as a street lamp shines its light onto the property. She told me that when the curtains are left open, she regularly sees a man walking through some of the rooms late at night. She also said sometimes she feels as though her privacy is being invaded as he stands in one of the windows of an upstairs room and stares across the road at her.

This revelation and the knowledge that someone, or something could be roaming the house while I was asleep, made me feel deeply uncomfortable in the property and I moved very soon after.

High Street, Tenterden
Emily P

In my family home, I experienced many paranormal events. The house itself was very large and old, having been built before the turn of the century. The house had been passed down from my grandparents to my parents when I was very young.

Even when I was young, strange things would happen in the house, such as items disappearing or being moved. We also heard weird noises throughout the house, but being so young, I never thought it could be a ghost or that something paranormal was taking place.

When I tried to speak to my parents about what was happening, or to my uncle who had lived in the house when he was a child, they would only say that strange things had happened to them too but would never elaborate or discuss things further.

The house had a large basement, consistomg of several rooms, mirroring the layout of the ground floor of the house. There was only one way into the basement, via a door in the kitchen. One of the rooms had been turned into a utility room, and it was here that I felt most uncomfortable. The room seemed to have a negative atmosphere and regularly had unexplained temperature changes. Sometimes I would also hear noises coming from this room even though nothing was switched on. No explanation could ever be found; my parents even hired a plumber and an electrician to find out what could be causing the problems, but they never found anything.

One experience I had was when my best friend and I were having a sleep over. My friend had suggested using her Ouija board to see if there were any spirits in the house. In those days, a Ouija board was hard to come by, so I jumped at the chance. My friend had obtained one during a recent visit to America and was keen to try it out with someone else. She had been too scared to use it on her own!

That evening, my mum needed to pick my brother up from one of his friend's house in a neighbouring village. As my dad was away on business, it meant we would be left on our own for about 20 minutes. She asked if we wanted to go with her, but we were keen to have the house to ourselves.

Once she had left, we went up to my room and my friend pulled her Ouija board out of her bag. We started moving the planchette around the board, seeing if we could communicate with anyone. About five minutes later, we heard the washing machine start in the utility room in the basement. Thinking my mum had come back to put the washing machine on, I called out to her that she should hurry up otherwise my brother would be waiting outside his friend's house for her. There was no answer. I called out again and still no answer came. Thinking my mum had left without hearing me, we carried on with the Ouija board.

After about ten minutes and having no success contacting anyone through the board, we gave up and went down to the kitchen to get some snacks. It was here that we noticed the door to the basement was ajar and all the lights were switched on down there. My friend and I stood at the top of the stairs leading down; being alone we were terrified.

Suddenly we saw someone cross in front of the stairs; it made us both jump backwards through fright. From the angle we had, we could only see the person from their feet up to just below the neck. It was clearly a woman, so I called out, "mum?" The response we got was "I'll be up in a minute".

Relieved, we grabbed some crisps and walked out of the kitchen into the hall, intending to go up the stairs. All of a sudden, the front door opened and my mum and brother walked into the house. Both my friend and I screamed. Seeing the fear on our faces, my mum asked what was wrong; we explained and as a group we ventured down into the basement, calling out for who was there.

We never did find anyone and to this day, still have no explanation other than it must have been a ghost.

College Avenue, Tonbridge
Clare T

My story concerns a house I lived in while I was at college. The house was built in the 1960's and was shared between me and Emily, another student at the college. We each had our own rooms but the rest of the house was shared. To give us some privacy and to increase security while we were out of the house, the landlord had added locks to each of our rooms, which could be secured with a padlock.

One evening, I was in my bedroom when I heard the front door open and close downstairs. I didn't think much of it at first, as I thought it was Emily returning home from her evening job at a local supermarket. I heard footsteps coming up the stairs and saw a glimpse the person walk past the gap in my door and go into Emily's bedroom.

I opened my door to go and say hello, but as I approached Emily's door, I noticed the door was shut and padlock still in place, firmly locked, even though there was no way the door could be locked like this when there was someone inside. I knocked on the door and called out for Emily but there was no response.

A little unnerved, I checked the house both upstairs and downstairs. All rooms were empty and the front door was still locked. There were no signs that anyone had come home. Perplexed, I went back upstairs to my room where I continued my coursework for the next day's lessons.

About an hour later, Emily did actually come home. I immediately went to her and asked if she had been home earlier that evening but gone back out. Emily had no idea what I was talking about and said she hadn't been home at all that day; she had only just finished work.

I explained what had happened, so we checked Emily's room together. Thankfully there was nothing out of place and didn't appear that anyone had been in the room. At this point, Emily turned to me and explained she too had heard footsteps and had seen someone briefly on the hall landing.

Since my first experience of the ghost, we've both continued to hear the sounds of phantom footsteps walking up the stairs and into one of the upstairs rooms.

Goldsmid Road, Tonbridge
Simon D

When I was in secondary school, we had a teacher who was a devout Christian; he was our RE (religious education) teacher and also our home teacher for the year. The home teacher is basically the teacher who is responsible for you for the year, to take the register and be the main person you go to with any problems. At the end of each year, you change to another teacher.

Being an all-boys school and being teenagers, most of us didn't take his RE lessons very seriously and we tried to disrupt them by getting him to go off subject. It was an opportunity to get bragging rights for the person who managed to get him off subject for the longest time.

Back in those days, smart phones or the internet didn't exist, the TV only had four channels and all we knew was what we read in books, newspapers, magazines or what we saw on the TV. In the local video shop, a friend of mine had seen a horror movie called the Exorcist. His parents hadn't let him rent it out much to his dismay and despite his pleading. He'd read the write up on the back of the VHS box so knew what the film was about. As we perceived this to be related to religion in some way, it was therefore fair game to use as a discussion point to get the teacher off subject.

It was very successful, the teacher spent nearly the whole of the lesson talking about the film the story and what the cause of the problems were; a Ouija board. Being in the UK, we'd never heard of these and were shocked to hear in America it was deemed a child's game and available in toy shops nationwide. We managed to get our teacher to describe the board, how they are used and what they are used for; basically to communicate with the dead. I don't think the teacher knew just how much information and instruction he had given us in that lesson, or how he had ignited our imagination about how we could communicate with a spirit to get whatever we wanted.

At the end of the lesson, the teacher finished his talk with a warning about how we should never use a Ouija board as they were evil, can't be controlled and would unleash the Devil on those who use it. The room full of young boys found this highly amusing and I don't think anyone took him seriously.

At play time, my friends, Dan, Simon, and Gareth all gathered round and we came up with a plan to meet up later that evening at Dan's house as only his older brother would be there. As we couldn't buy an Ouija board in the shops in this country, our intention was to draw our own on a piece of paper and use a glass as a planchette.

As planned, we met up and we each started to draw our own interpretation of what a board should look like. It was great fun and we spent most of the time laughing at each other's creation. Eventually, we chose the best one, Dan's, and agreed we would use that for our first communication with the unknown.

The main light in Dan's bedroom was turned off and only a small lamp on his desk illuminated the room. You could smell the nervousness in the room as we each placed the ends of our fingers on the upturned glass tumbler. We looked at each other and all burst out with a nervous laughter, each one of us unsure what we should do next. Remembering what our teacher had told us, we started moving the tumbler around the makeshift board and Gareth asked, "Is there anyone there?" Simon, ever the joker, let out an enormous fart, thinking it would be funny. Obviously it was and we started to crack up with laughter again, but almost immediately the glass tumbler flew up into the air from under our fingertips and hit the desk lamp with a crack and a shatter.

The tumbler broke into large shards of glass and the light bulb shattered into a million pieces; the room went pitch black and we immediately fell silent, no longer amused by Simon's toilet humour. I was so shocked by what had happened, my heart felt as though it would burst through my chest with how fast it was beating. I got up and put the main light on; there was shattered glass everywhere. Dan's brother came into the room to find out what the commotion was and helped us tidy up. As a group, we were quieter than we'd ever been. It was like we didn't want to talk about the fact that the glass tumbler had just defied gravity by flying upwards into the air with such force.

When the shock had gone, we all agreed it was probably best we didn't try messing with a Ouija board again, let alone disrespecting it as we had done that evening. We said our goodbyes and headed home; Simon on his own and Gareth with me as he lived in my road. As it was the winter, it was dark but the roads were well lit with the street lamps.

We were walking down the road and I spotted something move out of the corner of my eye. It had been in the reflection of a car window which was parked by the side of the road. I wasn't sure what I'd seen, but it definitely wasn't there now so I carried on walking down the road with Gareth. We walked past another parked car and I saw the movement in the reflection again. I stopped and told Gareth to look at the window.

In the reflection, we could see a shadow stood behind us. We weren't really sure what we were looking at, so we turned around but there was nothing there. We carried on at a quicker pace now, nervously looking around. Gareth suddenly pointed over to a house which had a large bay window. The curtains were shut but in the glass we could see two red glowing eyes. We carried on at a much quicker pace now, almost a jog, but as we did, we saw dark figures or red eyes watching us in reflections of cars, house windows and glass doors.

I looked behind me and saw that the street lamps were being shut off behind us, one at a time. The darkness seemed so black, no light could penetrate it. Terrified, we ran as fast as we could, matching each other's speed until we neared our own homes. We didn't stop to say goodbye, we just ran straight into our own homes and slammed the doors shut.

Thankfully nothing else happened that evening but the following day, Dan didn't come to school. He didn't return for several weeks either. He didn't return our calls and when I went to his house his mum said he wasn't seeing anyone at the moment. From that point, he was like a different person; very introverted and totally caught up in his own thoughts. He didn't talk to us very often and never hung out with us again. He refused to tell us why he was off or whether anything happened to him that night. When Gareth and I started to tell him about our experience, he started to cry and ran off.

I would advise anyone who is thinking of messing with a Ouija board to leave them well alone; it cost me one of my closest friends and I believe that had Gareth and I not run so fast, it could have cost me a lot more.

Greggs Wood Estate, Tunbridge Wells
Nick K

We live in a council owned house on the Greggs Wood estate in Tunbridge Wells. One night my mum got up to go to the toilet. She switched the light on, did what she needed to do and walked out of the room. As soon as she switched the light off, she heard something being dragged across the counter top in the bathroom and then there was a loud crash against the door behind her. She went back in and switched the light on to see what had happened.

What she found was that one of her candles, it was one of the posh ones in a large glass jar, had been smashed and the pieces of glass and candle were lying on the floor. The candle itself was too large and too heavy to be accidentally knocked over, and even if it did, it was impossible for the candle to leave the counter top and hit the door on its own.

Obviously scared, she quickly cleared up the mess, put it in a bag and went to put it in the bin in the kitchen. After this she went back to bed, but had trouble falling asleep as she had a terrible feeling as if she was being watched. It made her feel very uncomfortable. However some time later, she did eventually fall asleep.

In the morning, she felt a little better about the night's events and went to take a shower as she did every morning. However, when she pulled the shower curtain back, she discovered the broken glass and the remains of the candle from the previous night had been placed into the bath. She still has no idea how the pieces could have been taken out of the bag in the kitchen and put here, or how the candle was thrown and smashed.

Since that night, she is regularly woken up at different times during the night; she told me that it feels like someone has sat down on the edge of the bed; she can feel the bed move, but when she looks, there is never anyone there.

Happy Valley, Tunbridge Wells
"Janet"

Happy valley; the very name of this area close to Rusthall and Langton Green conjures thoughts of beautiful views of the Weald which can still be seen today, albeit through the trees which have obscured some of the view.

It is famous for Sweeps Cave; two alcoves carved into the local sandstone and were called this as they were used by local chimney sweeps to store soot. Another reason for the area's fame is the historic 105 steps down into the valley, which were originally built to provide access to the cold baths which are several hundred years old. However by the 1840's, the original steps had become covered by mud and grass and not revealed again until 1959 when the broken and missing steps were replaced. A sign stands at the top of the steps with a warning explaining how slippery the steps and banks of the valley become when they are wet.

This brings us to the legend of this unique place. In the 1830's, Sweeps Cave was nicknamed 'the dormitories for gypsies' following the publication of a town guide. If the stories are to be believed, one of the gypsies was walking through the area late at night when a thunder storm began. She hurried towards Sweeps Cave where she sheltered from the torrential rain. Once the storm had passed, she continued on her journey and attempted to walk down the hill, via the area where the 105 stairs had previously been covered with mud. As previously explained, this area was notoriously slippery when wet, which, to her dismay, she found out first hand. She had only just begun her descent down the hill, when she slipped in the mud, and tumbled all the way down the rest of the hill, breaking many bones on her journey to the bottom.

Isolated, bleeding and in terrible pain, she realised she was in desperate need of help; when her shouts of help went unanswered, she began dragging herself up the steep slope she had just fallen down. When she was about halfway up, she succumbed to her injuries and died. Her lifeless body was found the morning after; the mark where her shoe had slipped in the mud could still be seen, as could the trail of blood from the bottom of the hill up to where she had managed to pull her injured body.

Since this fateful day, stories have emerged of people hearing a woman calling for help late at night, particularly when the weather is bad. A few have reported the feeling of being pushed towards the edge of the valley when in the vicinity of the steps or along the top path, and others have spoken of strange shadows around the caves themselves and the feeling of being watched.

Perhaps the scariest incident which has been reported took place in late 2015. Much in the same way as the original story, a woman named Janet was heading down the stairs late one night, taking care as it had rained earlier that evening. She had been to the Beacon pub with her friends and was making her way home via a shortcut through Happy Valley. When she was about a quarter of the way down, she spotted movement further down the hill, just to the right of the steps. It was dark so she strained to see what it was; she initially thought it was a large animal, but as the shape came closer, she could see it was a woman pulling herself up the hill.

Ready to rush to the injured woman's aid, Janet suddenly noticed the woman's movements were strange and there seemed to be a weird black mist spiraling around her; it was as if the woman was gliding her way towards her. Janet explained to me that the woman appeared translucent and the grass around and under the body was not affected by the movements of the woman. When she saw this, Janet turned around and fled back up the stairs and to the Beacon where she told her friends. They immediately went back to the scene to investigate, but the woman could not be found and there was no evidence that the incident had ever taken place.

Silverdale Road, Tunbridge Wells
Gloria S

My story begins many years ago when I began my teaching career. I started working in an infant school in Tunbridge Wells called St Lukes. I worked here for some time before leaving. In recent years, the school was closed and sat unused but has now reopened as a nursery school after much renovation.

While I worked there, every morning the children would go outside for playtime, leaving the school empty apart from some of the teachers. One morning I was working at my desk in one of the classrooms when out of the corner of my eye I saw a young boy come into the room and stand by one of the desks.

Engrossed in what I was doing, I didn't look up but asked if I could help with anything. A moment passed and there was no answer so I looked up to find the room empty. I stood up and looked out of the classroom and into the hall, but again there was no one to be seen. I put this down to either the child running out of the room without me seeing, or there hadn't been anyone there and I'd just imagined it.

Later that day, at home time the children were leaving the classroom when one of the girls came up to my desk and asked who the new boy was, and why I hadn't introduced him. I asked the girl who she meant and she said, "the boy who had come into the room during the afternoon and had stood by that desk over there." She pointed over at the same desk where I thought I'd seen someone earlier that day. The girl continued to say, "he must be a fast runner because one moment he was there and then the next he was gone".

When all the children had gone home, I spoke to the head teacher of the school who looked concerned when I explained what had happened. It turned out other teachers had commented on catching a glimpse of a child in different areas of the school. Sometimes the sounds of a child playing would be heard in one of the classrooms, or one of the teachers would see a child through a window when they were outside in the play area. When they come into the school to investigate, no-one would be there.

It seems because they never got a good look at the child, they always put it down to their imagination, but since my experience, I know it was something more. Since that day, I kept a close eye on the girl who had stopped by my desk, often asking if she had seen the boy since, but she always said no. Although I haven't seen him again myself, sometimes when I come into the classroom in the morning, the seat for the desk he stood at is often pulled out when no others in the room are. It's as if he was sat at his desk waiting for lessons to begin.

Monson Road, Tunbridge Wells
Sarah E

My story dates back to the 1980's and a toy shop called White's Bazaar on Monson Road. The shop closed many years ago and I believe there is a hardware shop which has taken over the premises where the toy shop was. Although my story is quite old, I wouldn't be surprised if the current owners of the shop experience something of what we did.

When the toy shop was there, it had two floors; one on the ground floor and the other in the lower ground floor where you had to walk down an old wrought iron spiral staircase. There was always a bad vibe in the shop, both before it opened in the morning and particularly at night when we were closing. I suppose the joy and energy of children in a toy shop made things feel better during the day.

The first time I experienced the haunting was a Saturday in December. We had been very busy as people were preparing for Christmas. We had locked up and were dealing with the takings for the day when we heard a child crying down in the lower ground floor. This was followed by the sounds of a child running and then a muffled thud.

Thinking that there was still a customer here, I immediately went down the stairs calling out that the shop was closed. However, when I reached the bottom of the stairs, I couldn't find anyone. I did see a large box of Lego which had fallen onto the floor. Assuming this was the noise I put it back and went upstairs, believing the sound of the child was from outside.

Nothing else happened that evening, but we often would hear the sound of children downstairs. Each time we would check, there was no-one there except for random boxes of toys that had been moved or thrown onto the floor. None of the staff could explain it and we jokingly nicknamed the spook Legolas after a character from Lord of the Rings. We called him this as it was predominantly Lego boxes that was moved.

Something else that spooked me out was the doll and soft toy cabinet. In the entrance to the shop was a cabinet which had a glass front and contained dolls and teddy bears; they were locked away as some of them were quite expensive.

Several times, the dolls would be looking one way when we left for the night and when we returned in the morning the heads would have been turned towards the door. It was as if they had watched us leave and were waiting for us to return the next day. This was in the days before CCTV so we never found the true cause of this. We initially thought it was one of the staff who was playing a joke on us but it soon became obvious it was the dolls that were moving on their own.

One day my friend who also worked there, had become increasingly frustrated with the presumed joke and took one of the dolls out of the cabinet, put it back into its presentation box and took it out back into the store room. When she returned, we stood by the till for a while, discussing the situation when she looked up and screamed, then pointed to the cabinet.

I looked over and was shocked to see the doll, which she had taken to the store room, had returned and was sat amongst the soft toys looking at us! I rushed out back to look in the presentation box, but I couldn't find it.

My friend became increasingly obsessed with this doll and was convinced the dolls eyes were moving and would watch her when she was alone upstairs. She became so paranoid about the doll, that she actually bought it herself and locked it away in a box in her attic. She was too afraid of it to try and destroy it.

I personally don't think the doll was the problem, I believe it was something that was haunting the shop that moved the toys and dolls.

Grove Tunnel, Tunbridge Wells
Mike J

This story started when I was much younger. My dad was an engineer and worked at West Station in Tunbridge Wells. I remember being driven down to the bottom of the town to collect him after work, as it was usually quite late at night when he finished. After the railway and station had been closed down when I was twelve years old, he told me some stories of things that had happened in one of the tunnels.

The tunnel in question was Grove tunnel and sat in the far corner of the station. This tunnel was opened in 1876, so it's pretty old now. It used to have a single line rail track running through it with a signal box just outside. I think it was created to link the Hastings, Lewes and Eastbourne lines. The station and the railway were closed in 1985 and since then, a Sainsburys and Homebase have been built on the land. The station house is still there, but is now a pub and restaurant.

Back when my dad worked there, they used to have a problem with tramps and homeless people finding places to spend the night out of the cold and rain. They usually kept to the normal places of shelter and the guys working for the station would sometimes do a walk around the land and tracks and move them on. They'd always return though.

There came a point when some of the homeless people realised that Grove tunnel was the perfect place to spend the night. The main reason for this was that in the tunnel, there are safety points for the workers to take refuge when the trains come through. These are effectively recessed holes in the wall of the tunnel, but in Grove Tunnel, they are much larger than normal. These were therefore the perfect place for someone to make their overnight home out of the rain. The station workers were obviously concerned people may be in the tunnel and it was a big safety issue.

One day, the body of a homeless man was found in one of the recessed safety points. My dad was told that he was found sitting up, eyes wide open with a look of sheer terror on his face. From what I could get from my dad, there was never any explanation over how the man died. From that point on, the issue with homeless people accessing the tunnel stopped altogether; no-one else was ever found spending the night there.

A month or so went by with nothing out of the ordinary happening in the tunnel, but all that was about to change. Two workers (I don't know their names, but I'll call them Matthew and Ralph) were in the tunnel checking something, when there was a need to take shelter as a train was about to come through the tunnel. They had lamps or torches with them, I'm not sure which they used, so they easily found the safety recess; each person taking a different one to give themselves more room.

As the train was entering the tunnel, Ralph felt a strange sensation; the pressure around him changed and the atmosphere seemed to drip with cold (I know a lot of people will say this is because of a change in pressure due to the train approaching and entering the tunnel, but Ralph told my dad he'd never experienced anything like it). As the train was approaching the man, he felt as though he was being pinned down by something; he said it felt like two hands bearing down on his shoulders, pushing him down into the floor. The more terrifying feeling was when he felt the pressure start to push (rather than pull) him out of the safety recess. He had a real concern he would be pushed into the path of the oncoming train, so instinctively cried out and scrambled to keep himself in the recess as the train passed. The pressure stopped once the train had gone past.

Matthew came running over to him to see if he was OK Even in the light of the torches, Ralph could see the concern on Matthew's face, and seemed as shaken as he was. When Ralph explained what he had felt, Matthew looked shocked and explained how when the train was approaching, he looked over to where Ralph was and saw another man crawl into the recess with him.

Ralph was dumbfounded; there had been no-one there with him, all he had felt was the pressure which felt like two hands bearing down on him. When the two men returned to the station and spoke to the other workers, they joked it must have been the ghost of the homeless man wanting his alcove back. Matthew later gave Ralph a description of the man he saw. Even though there was limited light, Ralph said the man looked dishevelled and 'tramp-like', with a terrible look on his face.

From that point on, many workers felt strange things in the tunnel and there were reports of people being pushed, scratched and hit, the cause of which could never be explained. Towards the end of the station, repair and maintenance of the whole railway including Grove tunnel was reduced and eventually stopped, leading to poor conditions of the track beds. Due to this and the stations impending demise, the tunnel wasn't accessed very often.

Another story told to my dad was by someone who was doing some work in the signal box situated just outside the tunnel. He told my dad how he'd seen weird things in the mouth of the tunnel, sometimes appearing to be a person and then something like a swirling mist. He went to investigate but nothing could ever be found. This helped to perpetuate the belief that the tunnel was now haunted.

Since the station closed and the land redeveloped, the tracks have been removed. However, Grove Tunnel still exists behind the coach park and is accessible if you know where to go to get round the huge fence. There's graffiti as you would expect with an isolated area, but bizarrely it only exists in the mouth of the tunnel; as you go deeper, the vandalism stops.

The story of the homeless ghost has become a not very well known local legend in the bottom end of the town, and some of the teenagers from the estates near the tunnel see it as a sort of rite of passage to spend time in the safety recesses. I've heard a few of them talk about how they've had similar experiences and have literally been assaulted by an unseen force while in the tunnel.

Blackhurst Lane, Tunbridge Wells
Gordon T

A couple of years ago, I was in a relationship with a girl and as we both lived with our parents, we found it hard to get time together alone. Getting time together with no-one else around would usually involve driving somewhere and parking up, or going to a pub somewhere out of the way.

One night, we had parked up in a lane in Tunbridge Wells, just outside of the town. The lane itself leads nowhere, and if you go all the way to the end, it just abruptly stops as it has been blocked off. At some point in the distant past it obviously led somewhere. I think it may have been closed when the A21 was built. It's quite a dark road, the street lights are few and far between and the further you drive down it, the darker it gets. When we stopped here, it was the beginning of December and the winter night had drawn in early, but due to the lack of clouds in the sky, the road was illuminated by the moon with its eerie glow.

We were just chatting in the car and enjoying each other's company, the interior was illuminated by the glow of the radio and dashboard. Although it was a cold night, we had the windows open a little bit to prevent them from steaming up (not that we were doing anything like that!). I was in the driving seat, Amy was in the passengers seat and we were sat facing each other with our backs to the car doors. The car itself was parked on the right-hand side of the road as there was a parking or passing spot in the lane, so basically facing oncoming traffic, not that there was any.

The lane where we were parked has a field on the left side and woods on the right. Above the sound of the radio, we could hear the creaking of the trees and the blowing of the wind through the branches and whatever leaves remained on the trees. So at this point, it was just noises you would normally expect to hear when you are parked next to some woods.

After we had been there for a while, from behind me deep in the woods, I could just make out some noises which were out of place. It started with distant crunching of leaves. By this time of the year, the trees had mostly shed their leaves and whatever was left, were dropping. As it hadn't rained for a while, the leaves were dry and would crunch and break apart when you walked on them. This was the sound I was starting to hear; a crunch, crunch noise which sounded like someone walking around in the woods, treading on the dried leaves. It seemed as though it was a distance away but it was still quite distinctive. I looked over my shoulder into the woods and couldn't see anything; when I looked back, Amy was looking as well; she'd obviously heard the noise too.

We sat there for a while listening, when Amy broke the silence by saying, "It sounds like an animal walking around out there". I agreed and said, "It's probably a badger or a fox, would you like to stay or shall we make a move?" Amy wanted to stay so we continued listening and making suggestions of what the animal could be.

After a couple of minutes, the noises seemed to be getting closer, we looked out of the window again to see if we could see anything in the dark woods. All of a sudden, Amy looked startled and whispered, "look over there by that big tree, I think I saw something move". I looked over and to start with, couldn't see anything because the moonlight didn't permeate into the woods very well. Due to the dashboard lights, my eyes hadn't adjusted very well to the darkness, so I switched off the car completely, closed my eyes for a moment to get them accustomed to the complete darkness and looked into the woods in the direction of the big oak tree.

At first, all I could see were grey tree trunks, shadows jumping about from where the trees were swaying and that was pretty much it. The crunching noises had stopped and I was starting to think it was nothing other than our over active imaginations. Then a shaped moved away from the oak tree, completely black, darker than the blackness of the wood; it moved around the tree and behind another. The crunching sounds had started again, somewhat faster this time, but also accompanied with what sounded like an echo of wood hitting wood. Based on the sounds and the direction the shape had moved, it was clear whatever the thing was, it was heading towards the lane somewhere in front of the car.

Although the combination of moonlight, darkness, shapes moving about and strange noises spooked us, we both agreed it was probably a deer; the shape was definitely larger than a badger and certainly not a fox. We sat in silence as we saw about 100 yards up the lane, the thing stepped out onto the tarmac with a "clip clop", sounding very much like horses hooves would. It definitely wasn't a deer. I would describe it as a 'beast', and although it was dark, we still got a good look thanks to the moonlight.

It was upright, on its hind legs, I didn't get a very good look at its feet, so I can't say for certain what caused the "clip clop" noise. Its legs were skinny and it was hunched over. It seemed to have a large hunch around its shoulders; the chest was huge and tapered down into a very skinny waist. It wasn't a human face; it was more like a dog with what I thought were large ears sticking upright. It didn't have a tail that I could see and it seemed to have some sort of fur over its body.

It started to cross the lane to enter the field on the other side but about half way across it came to a stop and slowly turned its head to face us. I don't know whether it was the visual remnants of looking at the lights from the dashboard, but I swear to god its eyes burned red. It sounds ridiculous and like something you'd see in a horror movie, but both Amy and I saw it.

It stood there looking at us and we sat in the car looking back into what can only be described as a vision from hell. Its mouth opened in what I believe was a grin and with that, it turned its head and continued across the lane and over into the field. I didn't hang about, as soon as it was out of sight I started the car and floored it up the lane. Amy was in tears and took some time to calm down; I was shaking and I think we were both in shock of what we saw.

We've never told anyone else this story, I've always thought it sounds too crazy for anyone to believe us, but there's been some other stories in the news of weird creatures being spotted in

Tunbridge Wells and the surrounding areas so maybe my story isn't so far-fetched after all.

The Bull Inn, West Malling
Alan T

A few years ago, I was contacted by the management of The Bull Inn to hear the accounts of paranormal activity taking place on the premises. All the staff had experienced strange events throughout the premises and thought it would be useful to touch base with someone who investigates paranormal activity. At the time, some of the staff were quite concerned about their experiences and also the stories and tales being told by regulars of the pub, so the management team thought I would be able to provide a certain degree of reassurance.

The management advised the Inn was built in 1426 and it is believed there are links to the nearby Abbey, with rumours that one of the tunnels from the Abbey is linked to the Inn. However, this cannot be proven as the management have attempted to contact the Abbey regarding this, but to no avail. An extension was built in 1995 which doubled the size of the bar and added toilets at the rear.

In the cellar, unusual noises have been heard that cannot always be explained (this occurred while the interview was taking place) and when working alone down there, staff have had a feeling of being watched. Equipment failure within the bar has been a regular issue, for instance the soft drinks dispenser has stopped working and upon examination of the equipment and pipes, there appeared to be no fault. When staff tried to use the equipment again, it worked perfectly.

The pipes into the bitter barrels have also been pulled above the level of the bitter in the barrel several times, meaning the flow of liquid is interrupted and needs to be physically pushed back down (something else which happened while the interview was taking place). One of the staff members told me she observed through a crack in the floorboards a figure passing by in the cellar, but upon investigation, it was empty. Bangs and scraping (like someone not picking their feet up when they walk) have also been heard.

In the restaurant on the ground floor, different witnesses have regularly seen a lady dressed in white walking towards the rear of the room; she is usually seen from an aperture in the bar area.

Although the next haunting is not within the pub itself, it can sometimes be observed from the stairway leading to the first floor. When looking out of the window on the stairs, on occasion, an old lady laden with a hessian sack can be seen walking up the railway tracks. After a short distance, the lady disappears and there is no evidence of her ever being there. Another tale involving this window is that if you look at the window from outside, you may see the face of a young lady looking back at you. This happened to one staff member on the way into work one day, so they rushed in thinking someone had gained entry to the pub, only to find the place empty except for the manager. They checked the whole of the pub over, but could not explain who the woman was, or where she had gone.

Within the living area on the first floor, there is what is referred to as 'a void' between two walls. A mirror covered the majority of this at the time of the interviews so it couldn't be examined in detail. Staff advised there is a feeling of oppression when looking into the mirror and they occasionally see a dark shape moving behind them in the reflection. I was told that when the dark shape is witnessed, you can also hear scratching coming from behind the mirror in the void.

In what was being used as an office on the first floor, the manager reported he has in the past heard footsteps following him into the office, but when looking behind him, there was no one there.

On the first floor hallway/landing, a lady wearing a long black coat/cloak has been seen walking across the landing towards the bathroom. It is believed that this is the ghost of a nun. Creaking of floorboards could also be heard at the same time. As with similar events within the pub, when checking and looking for the person, no-one could be found.

In the first floor bedroom, the manager awoke one night at approximately 4am to hear childish giggling coming from downstairs in the bar area. He immediately he went to investigate but when he got to the fourth step from the bottom the giggling stopped.

Undeterred, he continued to investigate but could not find anyone, all the doors were locked and there was no apparent way anyone could exit the building.

Each of the two bedrooms upstairs have en-suite bathrooms. In one of them, a staff member told me the bathroom door frequently opens by itself, even though she had ensured it was safely shut. During the interview, I had an opportunity to examine this door. It is not able to open by itself, as the catch is secure and tight. If the catch is not latched correctly, the door does not open or shut on its own accord as the hinges were quite stiff.

It appears the regular patrons also have a wealth of knowledge, both about the hauntings and also about the previous residents of The Bull Inn, but it would seem they have resisted providing information to the current management. However, from what the staff have gleamed from them is that a previous worker caused himself self-inflicted wounds without knowing what he was doing whilst within the bar area. The patrons indicated to staff there's more to the hauntings that it seems, but were unwilling to discuss or provide any more clarification over what they meant. A few comments have been heard about 'something terrible' happening about 25-30 years ago, but again when questioned they wouldn't give further information.

As the interview was ending, one of the staff members mentioned sometimes she felt as though she is being held around the neck in certain areas of the Inn. Once this was divulged, all members of staff agreed with her. They also commented that sometimes it felt as though they were being pulled or pushed towards the main doors of the Inn.

Lower Road, Woodchurch
Sandy R

there have been some strange occurrences happening in our house. My husband and I moved into the house in 2002 and we lived there for over ten years without any problems, but recently some strange things have been happening which I can't explain.

The first time I had an experience which I would say was paranormal was when I was sitting in my living room with my sister who had come over to spend an evening with us. I was talking to my sister who was sitting in an armchair next to the door which leads to the hallway where our stairs to the 1st floor are. I saw something moving in the hallway behind her, so I turned my head to look thinking it was my husband, only to see a shadow walk down the hallway from one side of the door to the other. I asked my sister if she saw anything and she said she hadn't as she wasn't paying attention to the hall. At the time I assumed it was just shadows from a car headlight as the front door in the hallway has glass panels and basically forgot about it. However, after everything else that's happened, I would now consider this a paranormal event.

Over the next few weeks, things started getting even stranger. Literally everyday I would see shadows moving or floating around the house. Sometimes I would look and the shadows would just cross the room in front of me and disappear. Other times I would stare at one and it would just float off. The shadows would always appear in different shapes and sizes and it seemed as though they were getting bolder as it didn't seem to matter whether I was in the room with them.

My husband swore he hadn't seen anything and other visitors to the house seem unconcerned. I'm sure they were starting to worry about my sanity!

One night I had been watching Downton Abbey on the telly and my husband had gone to bed as it really wasn't his type of programme. When it had finished and I was going up to join my husband, I turned the corner at the top of the stairs and saw a shadow glide into our bedroom. Almost immediately I heard what sounded like my my husband cry out in pain. Although frightened, I ran into the room only to find him in a deep sleep. I woke him up and told him what I had seen, but he had no idea what I was talking about. There was no sign of injury on him and he had no recollection of being in pain or crying out. He said he must've had a bad dream, so we got into bed and settled down.

It took some time as I was unsettled but I was starting to drop off to sleep when I was startled by a pressure on my bed, down near my feet. It felt like there was someone sitting on the edge of my bed. Then I started to hear a noise that sounded like laboured, heavy breathing. It sounded like someone with a severe chest infection; it had a gurgling sound which caught as it took a breath. I was so afraid, and I held onto my husbands hand and shut my eyes tightly, afraid to look and see what it was. I could hear my husband next to me breathing slowly in his sleep, so it definitely wasn't him. After about 30 seconds it stopped and I looked to see nothing there.

Since then, I've been woken many times to the feeling of something sitting on my bed or the sight of something human shaped standing over by the window. I've heard stories like this where the person has been attacked, but thankfully I've never been and whatever it is, it seems happy to watch and co-exist with us. My husband still thinks I'm crazy though!

Closing Thought

Thank you for reading Ghosts in the Garden of England. I hope you've enjoyed hearing about the paranormal experiences of some of the people of Kent.

If you too have experienced something which couldn't be explained, then please get in contact with me! I would love to hear your story and perhaps you could feature in a future book!

You can contact me at: myghoststory@yahoo.com

Best regards

Alan Tigwell

Printed in Great Britain
by Amazon